TRIUMPHANT!

One Woman's Journey from Prison to Purpose

2019!

"It's important that we share our experiences
with other people.
Your story will heal you
and your story will heal somebody else.
When you tell your story, you free yourself
and give other people permission
to acknowledge their own story."

-Iyanla Vanzant

TRIUMPHANT!

One Woman's Journey from Prison to Purpose

Jessica Roberts

COPYRIGHT

Book Cover Photography by L. Devlin Photography

The Butterfly Typeface Publishing
PO BOX 56193
Little Rock Arkansas 72215

Dedication

To my daughter Shyla aka my ScooterPeas!!!

I prayed to God that our bond remains unbreakable. You were 23 months old when Mommie's life got turned upside down. You were so young and innocent but so calm and poised while witnessing your mom fall apart as the authorities took you from my arms.

As I cried and screamed, "No what did I do," I looked up and just knew you would be screaming and crying too. But to my surprise, you were calm and just stared at me. Our eyes locked on one another and you gave me the biggest smile. If I had to put your gaze and smile into words, it was like you were saying, "Geesh, Mommie. Get it together; I'm ok."

Instantly my tears and screams stopped.

That same strength and tenacity God implanted in me, I saw in you that day. A blessing from God is what you are my little *mini-me.*

I will never forget your amazing gaze that day because it reminded me of my strength. This book is dedicated you.

You are my everything, and my everything is you.

I love you!!

"My Broken Pieces"

I've been cut left, I've been cut right,
and even down the middle of my heart,
but yet there lied a flawless Master Piece
underneath all my Broken Pieces.

God healed my Broken Pieces
and helped me to see:

-the joy in the pieces
-the happiness in the pieces
-the peace of mind in the pieces
-the healing in the pieces.

I discovered and fell in love
with my broken pieces, ya'll.

The Peacemaker; the Mind Regulator;
the Heart Healer; the Soul Saver
took all my pieces and planted within me
a sense of peace beyond all understanding
and made me whole again.

The struggles from my Broken Pieces was the
super glue needed to create God's masterpiece.

My love for Life began from My Broken Pieces!

-Jessica Roberts

"Believe in yourself and all that you are.
Know that there is something inside you
that is greater than any obstacle."

Christian D. Larson

Table of Contents

Foreword

I am a woman filled with a compassion for helping others. I'm a humanitarian by nature.

From the time I was a child, I was known as a 'nice person' with a 'good heart.'

I knew that I was different, but I didn't come to understand and appreciate my uniqueness until God used them to reveal my gifts for the calling and purpose He had for my life.

I am a person who doesn't give up!

This 'never give up' spirit was planted in me as a child by my father. It began the day he taught me to ride my bike without the assistance of training wheels.

On this particular day, I was so excited to learn to ride my bike, but after one fall and a bloody, scraped kneed, I wanted to give up and go inside.

But my father wasn't having it.

I cried and screamed profusely in protest, but Dad wouldn't budge.

I fell again on that same bloody, scraped knee about four more times and still my father wouldn't allow me to quit.

Finally, after the fourth fall, I got the hang of it and was riding that bike like a pro.

Excited with glee, I ran inside to tell my mom the good news and to show her my war wound (the bloody, scrapped knee) as proof.

"Triumphant!" is filled with the experiences, choices, and situations I found myself in that caused hurtful wounds and made me want to give up, but I kept going.

Wounds don't stop me. They actually prepare me!

Acknowledgments

Writing a book was easier than I thought and more rewarding than I could have ever imagined. None of this ever would have been possible without the spiritually-grounded, positive, encouraging and influential people God allowed me to cross paths with throughout my life's *triumphant* journey. They've stood by me during every struggle and all my successes. And for this, I'm eternally grateful.

A very special thank you to my one and only daughter Shyla Nicole Alvin. You are my heartbeat, the love of my life. You are my reason for not giving up. Having you in my life helped me remain grounded, focused and determined. I'll always remain a soldier on this battlefield of life because I have you. I thank God for blessing me with you Scooterpeas.

To my mother and father thank you both for instilling morals and values in me. I'm grateful for the love, discipline, tough love, manners, respect, and so much more. All of which helped me turn my tragedy into triumph and succeed in life.

To Mrs. Sandra Smith (The Re-Entry Connection), thank you for extending me the invite to attend a Re-Entry Connection Group Meeting. Although it took a year before I finally attended, it was one of the greatest decisions I ever made. I'm forever grateful for your persistence. You taught me the importance of Mentorship and being a part of a Group. We are kindred spirits when it comes to having compassion for people and contributing to different causes to make the world a better place. Thank you for your listening ear when I needed to vent and for taking the time to pray with me/for me during my trying times. Thank you for appointing me as CFO of The Re-Entry Connection. The Re-Entry Connection has helped me more than words can express. Lastly, a big thank you and much love to the members and board members of The Re-Entry Connection you ladies are appreciated.

Finally thank you to my inner circle of family, friends & positive influencers, etc: Shontae Roberts (sister), Crystal Boyd (best friend), Minister Walker (Spiritual Mentor Louisville, Ga county jail), Jumpin Joe (friend/business partner), Author Sherena Frazier (friend), Sheneatra McCoy (friend), IsIs Flagg (friend), Nikki Williams (friend), Mistrell Alvin (Shyla's father), and Mike Jones (friend).

Writing a book about the story of my life has been a surreal process. Thank you to Iris M. Williams (Butterfly Typeface Publishing) for her editorial help, keen insight, and ongoing support in bringing my story to life. It is because of her efforts and encouragement that I have a legacy to pass on to my daughter/family where one didn't exist before.

Prologue

MY MOM AND DAD are the best parents anyone could ask for. In my eyes, they are the world's greatest! The love, morals, and values they instilled in me prepared me for life. They not only taught me those things, but they showed me how to be them. I consider those standards to be my most valuable assets and no doubt are what helped me get through the most difficult time of my life.

There was a seed planted in me long before I came into this world. As I was growing in my mother's womb, God had a plan for my life. He made sure that I'd have everything I needed in order to do everything He created me to do.

I tried to live my life the way I'd been shown, and early on, it wasn't as hard to do. But as I got older, choices weren't so black and white. Love can make you do things that you otherwise would not do.

Haven't you ever done something that you really didn't want to do, but it was for someone you really loved?

I've come to understand that sometimes, the places we find ourselves and the experiences we encounter serve to prepare us for our purpose.

Now that I have the benefit of age, experience, and wisdom, I can see how the things I went through has shaped the woman I am now. The dreams and goals I have now were not the dreams I started out with.

My love and my choices left me facing a ten-year prison sentence!

In spite of my choices and what I thought I wanted for my life, my dreams took a different turn. My new dreams have been directly influenced by the direction my life took.

Coincidence?

Read my story and then you can decide.

All Eyes On Me

WITH THE EXCEPTION of my best friend Cassidy, I'm not the type of person who has 'friends.' I'm more of an 'associates' type of person. It's how I've always been. I'm a loner. I don't like a lot of crowds or drama. I hung out and talked on the phone occasionally, but there was definitely a boundary around me. I didn't share my life with too many people.

"Let's skip school," Pam said. "They are showing a rated R movie at the Cinema, and I've been dying to see it!"

The other girls all agreed and were even excited about it, but not me.

"Nah," I said desperately trying to come up with a believable excuse. "I don't have any extra cash."

Rosa rolled her eyes. She was the most daring of our group. "Who said anything about paying Jessica!"

The other girls rolled their eyes and laughed.

The peer pressure was real!

Skipping school, sneaking into the movies, drinking, smoking, and having sex with boys were the types of things my 'associates' did. They were all daring and adventurous, but I just didn't want to do any of those things.

The older people would often say I was mature for my age and had an 'old soul,' but my peers just called me scary or chicken.

I often questioned myself and wondered if something was wrong with me for not wanting to participate in what seemed to be *normal* teenage antics.

It bothered me to be different.

Why do I have to be weird? Why can't I just be like all the other kids my age?

Don't get me wrong; I wasn't perfect or anything. I just didn't' want to act like or take part in a lot of the things kids my age were doing. I became known as the 'good girl.' I didn't sleep around, and I followed my parents' rules. I knew there would be consequences if I didn't, and I didn't want to pay them.

I didn't like the spotlight, but somehow, I always found myself there.

"Class, I want you to listen up," Mr. Mayo, our history teacher said. "I want to recognize Jessica for offering to help with the elementary school kids graduation program. She has also agreed to tutor them during the summer."

Of course, all eyes were on me, and of course, I wanted to disappear. I was popular, but not for the things that other girls my age were popular for; I was popular for being friendly, nice, and not easy when it came to boys.

Even back then I somehow had a sense of right and wrong, and it served me well.

I don't know what happened to my compass. All I know is making good choices became harder and harder.

Cassidy

CASSIDY AND I had been friends since our elementary school days. We met in 4th grade, and the bond was instant. We would dress alike, spend lots of time together, and share secrets. She was a kindred spirit and more like a sister to me than my two blood sisters. We knew each other's likes and dislikes when it came to hair, clothing, and boys.

Although we had so much in common, a two-parent home, for example, there were also areas where we were different. And so, while we understood each other, we also accepted each other. Over the years, others befriended me, but I always backed off because there was never a bond like the one Cassidy and I shared.

"I know you were lying today when Pam suggested we skip school," Cassidy said shaking her long hair. She knew me better than anyone else.

"Do you think they knew too?" I asked. Suddenly not so confident in my lying abilities. I shared things with her that I didn't share with others.

"Yea," Cassidy laughed. "It was lame, but who cares. You gotta do what you think is best for you."

That was one thing I appreciated about Cassidy. Her attitude toward life was, "Do what you feel you need to do."

Cassidy was sweet, short, thick and very cute. Her personality was fun. Sometimes our ideas weren't the same. I think she was rebelling against her mom's extreme religious views, which is probably why she never judged or questioned me. She also never got angry with me about the choices I made. That laid-back attitude clearly came from her father. He was a nice man, the bread-winner for the family, and spoiled her (not in a bratty way), but Cassidy didn't want for anything!

Cassidy and I experienced so much together.

She and I were driving before the legal driving age. Her father would allow us to drive his Pontiac Grand Am without any adult supervision to run errands, but of course, we went places outside of the assigned errand destination.

I told you I wasn't perfect!

The secrets I shared with Cassidy, I knew I couldn't share with anyone else.

"I think Dewayne is so fine," I confessed to Cassidy. "But he wants to –." I stopped and began clearing my throat when my sister walked into the room.

Cassidy and I had what we called a phone code, meaning whenever we were talking on the phone, and someone walked by or came into the room we were in, we would clear our throats twice to warn one another to change the subject of conversation because someone was present.

"Lil sis in the room huh?" Cassidy laughed.

"Yea," I said and watched her slow down to wait for me to continue what I was saying. "I can't believe Mr. Mayo gave us so much homework on a holiday weekend."

"Ugh," my sister groaned. She knew I'd changed the subject. "I don't know any dirt on you."

And she was right!

I learned at an early age not to share *any* of my secrets with either one of my sisters because as soon as one of them got mad at me for whatever reason; they would snitch to my mom and dad.

Even then I kept my circle of friends small. I knew a lot of people, but I didn't hang out with a lot of them – especially females. Females were quick to befriend me, but those friendships never lasted because we usually never had anything in common or they were jealous, all while calling me their 'friend.'

Basically, there was no connection.

For most of my life, I only had three friends outside of Cassidy.

I was determined to stay focused. I had plans and wanted to work hard to make my dreams come true. I wasn't interested in doing what the crowd was doing.

Somehow, the more I tried to stay under the radar, the more attention I seemed to bring to myself.

Kevin

I WAS IN THE 10TH GRADE when I had my first real relationship. His name was Kevin, and at the time he was everything I wanted: tall, slender, good hair, big pretty eyes, and mixed. His parents were black and Puerto Rican.

Kevin attended the rivalry high school. He was popular there and played on the basketball team. We met through his cousin Brad who attended the same school as me. It was at an after-school event where I saw Kevin for the first time.

"Go talk to him," Cassidy urged.

"NO," I hissed back at her. "That's never gonna happen."

My mentality was that a girl shouldn't approach a guy first even if she liked him. She had to wait for him to approach her. Although Kevin didn't approach me that day, I did catch him staring at me several times.

The next day at school, Kevin's cousin approached me.

"Hey Jessica," Brad said grinning. "I got something for you."

It was a note from Kevin:

Hey sweet thang

Call me when you get this note

Kevin 555-222-3333

I phoned Kevin two days later, and we had a great conversation. He shared with me how he felt like he had to be the man of the house since it was just him and his two brothers. He confessed he never knew his dad and my heart went out to him. That and the fact that he was a basketball player too, made me like him even more!

After conversing on the phone several times a day for about a month, Kevin and I decided to make it official and became girlfriend and boyfriend. I was fifteen years old, and because of my parents' rule, I was only able to talk to him on the phone. I couldn't go out on dates until I was sixteen.

Of course, I got to see Kevin at basketball games, the mall, local events, and parks, so my parents' rule wasn't hard to abide by. Although Kevin's upbringing was very different from mine, he went along with my parents' rules and didn't give me a hard time about them.

I was in love.

When I turned sixteen, Kevin and I were still a couple. I was now driving and dating legally.

Every free moment I had was spent with Kevin. He was either at my house, or I was at his. Kevin made me feel as though I was the apple of his eye.

The first two years of our relationship was heavenly.

Then Kevin went from being the love of my life to a person I didn't recognize.

But I made the choice to stay with him thinking that my loving and sound upbringing influence would change him back to the person he was when we first met.

Nothing could have been further from the truth.

The Change

BY THE TIME we were juniors in high school, Kevin had started hanging out with the wrong crowd. He began missing school and eventually dropped out and began working full-time as a dishwasher. Working as a dishwasher exposed Kevin to lots of bad habits such as smoking cigarettes and drinking.

I didn't understand his decisions, but by making the choice to stay with him, I guess in some way I supported his bad habits.

Kevin and I came from two different worlds. A lot of the things he could get away with at home, I wouldn't dare try!

Kevin was raised by a single, working mom while I was being raised in a two-parent home, maybe this was the difference, I'm not sure, but education was of extreme importance in my household.

I continued with school but worked a part-time job at a hardware store. I chose not to tell my parents that Kevin dropped out of school because I knew they would have made me break up with him.

Kevin had also developed a bad temper and drinking only intensified it.

"Hey Kevin," I said happily as I walked into his bedroom. "What you doing?"

"What does it look like I'm doing?" He said as he lay on his bed with his arms behind his head.

The TV was on, but he didn't seem to be watching it.

"Looks like you're being lazy," I said, trying to make a joke and ease the tension.

"Not everyone is a super girl like you," he said sarcastically.

I could smell the alcohol on his breath and knew this situation wasn't going to get any better, so I decided it was best to leave.

"Well, I'm gonna go," I said. "I see you're not in the mood for company."

He jumped off the bed and blocked the doorway. "You're not going anywhere."

"Ok," I said. Now I was scared. I sat down on the bed, and he just stood there for a while staring at me.

"I'm gonna go grab another beer," he said.

As soon as he left the bedroom, I made a run for the door. I heard Kevin running behind me, but I kept going until I made it to my car. I managed to unlock the door and get in, but before I could close it, Kevin positioned himself between me and door so that I couldn't close it.

"Move Kevin," I cried. "You're scaring me."

But instead of moving, he put both his arms around my neck and began choking me. I tried my best to fight him off, but I couldn't.

By this time, I was beyond terrified. And all I could think to do was scream.

A neighbor yelled, "Stop. Don't kill her!"

She ran across the street to my rescue and begged Kevin to stop, and he eventually did. The neighbor held Kevin's attention just long enough for me to sit back down in the car, but just as I was about to close the door, he snatched the door handle. I reached to grab the door away from him as one of my legs hung out of the car but missed. This angered him, and he slammed the door closed on my leg.

I screamed to the top of my lungs, frightening him long enough so that I was able to get away.

I was so upset, but I made the choice not to tell anyone, not even my best friend, Cassidy.

That was the first time of many that Kevin physically put his hands on me.

I cried myself to sleep that night.

The next day I awoke to a huge painful bruise on my leg. And of course, Kevin contacted me with excuses and apologies. I saw him later that evening, and he apologized. There were tears in his eyes. I forgave him unaware that this was the start of a cycle of physical abuse.

As long as he wasn't drunk, Kevin and I had good times together. We traveled to amusement theme parks, attended events together in town and out of town.

One thing about Kevin he was good at wining and dining me. I was always getting roses on and off the job, dinner and movie dates, the works.

Looking back, I guess he had to do these things to keep my mind off the toxic person he really was.

Isolation

I **GRADUATED** from high school and continued my relationship with Kevin.

I chose to attend the local Community College because I didn't want to be far away from him. I rationalized that decision by telling myself that I wasn't selling myself short by going to Community College because while it wasn't my first choice, it was still college.

There I was excited. I was in my first year of college and working a full-time job. A few people I knew from high school and the rivalry high schools were in attendance at the college as well. I had a few associates I talked and hung out with sometimes, but Cassidy who didn't attend college, was still my best friend.

I was the only one in my group of associates who had a car, so I often gave them rides to their jobs or home. And I never asked for gas money.

My relationship with Kevin got worse as time went on. He didn't like me hanging out with *any* college associates and insisted that my free time was spent with him.

He often worked at night, so I still hung out and did things, I just didn't tell him. After attending college for a year, I became more interested in the Dental Assistant Program offered there, and in my second year, I enrolled. There were only females enrolled in the Dental Program at this time, and I was the only African American student.

I was excited about my journey into Dental Assisting, that is until I was assigned an internship that revealed my race could be an issue.

"Are you the only African American in the program?" The Dentist asked.

"Yes," I replied.

"I figured as much," she went on to say. "When your school's program director called to inquire about the internship, she asked me if I had an issue working with a black student."

What the program director didn't know was that she was speaking to a dentist who was also an African American female.

I tried to view this situation in a positive light by considering that the Program Director had my best interest at heart and didn't want to place me in an uncomfortable situation, but it was hard. I developed a strong dislike for the School Program Director. Every time I saw her, I had minimal to say, and my expression was like I smelled something stink.

I thought, *how could she be a racist and she's a lesbian? She should know first-hand what it feels like to be discriminated against.*

Although I struggled with the dental anatomy class and thoughts of the program director's seemingly racist actions, I continued with the program.

In addition to being a full-time dental assistant student, I also worked a full-time job. After my second internship, which was in oral surgery, I quickly learned that the medical field was not for me. I found out I had a weak stomach. I continued with the program for a few months longer and decided I no longer wanted to be a Dental Assistant.

My father was so disappointed in me which hurt me to the core, but I was an adult, and I knew that I had made the right choice for me.

Although Kevin was a constant source of stress for me during the entire time I was in the program, he supported my decision to quit, and that offered me some comfort.

It didn't occur to me that maybe he was only supportive of my quitting because it kept me isolated.

Yearning For More

I APPLIED AND STARTED working for a well-known bank as a bank teller. I worked the bank's drive-thru window (the commercial and personal banking side). I absolutely loved this job. I was very likable amongst most of the staff and the customers.

Although, Kevin and I were still a couple, that didn't stop the men from pursuing me.

I remember one Valentine's Day in particular.

Kevin and I had had an argument, and we weren't speaking so imagine my surprise when I got not just one delivery, but three!

"And here is another delivery for you Ms. Jessica," Raymond the security guard said with a grin.

"OOOOOh," Samantha squealed. "Let me see the card."

She grabbed it before I could stop her.

"And yep, this one's from a different man too!" She revealed, and the whole bank seemed to laugh.

I was uncomfortable with the attention from my coworkers, but I have to admit it felt good to be pursued.

"If one more delivery comes through that door for you," Fred the branch manager said, "I'm leaving for the day."

It really was a sight to see. There were candy, balloons, and roses everywhere.

Not everyone was gushing over my deliveries like I was. Vivian, an older lady, had a hard time hiding her jealousy. "Gosh Jessica," she said tightly. "You're going to need to take those to the back. They're blocking the cameras."

I had to get help taking them to the breakroom and again when I took them to my car later when my shift was over. Since I still lived at home with my parents, Kevin didn't know, and I never told him.

I must admit that was a Valentine's Day to remember. The attention was good, but I knew there was more to life and I desired for it personally as well as professionally.

A few months later I applied, and I got a position within the bank's Retail Operation Center. I was now Lockbox Specialist. My main responsibilities included processing the customers' lockbox payments and processing overdraft charges.

I left the front banking scene for the back scene (banking operations). I was so excited about the change and the opportunity to learn something new that would make me more of an asset to the company and add more employment experience to my resume.

Working as a Lockbox Specialist afforded me the opportunity to see and learn how banking transactions are processed once they leave the teller line. I loved the challenges that came with this position. Analyzing, researching and finding resolutions excited me and stretched my brain cells so-to-speak.

I loved this job but, yet my mind and soul yearned for more.

Deja Vue

AFTER BEING OUT of high school for nearly two years, I decided to pursue my Associate degree. Working a full-time job and attending Community College part-time kept me busy, but it was an exciting time for me. I felt I was finally on my way to my dream career.

As happy as I was professionally, my personal life was in shambles. My relationship with Kevin was on its last legs. The more I focused on my career and education the clearer it became to me that Kevin and I weren't compatible. All we had between us were a lot of years.

Don't get me wrong, our entire relationship wasn't all bad, but I was outgrowing him and knew in my heart that he wasn't the one.

After my third college semester, I decided to break up with Kevin. Yes, after 9 ½ years of ups and downs, I was finally walking away. I must admit it was bittersweet because I'd gotten very comfortable with him. So, I missed him, but it was quite refreshing not having the weight of trying to keep him happy while pursuing my goals too. I realize my heart had left months prior; it just took my mind a little time to agree with my heart.

A few months after the breakup, I decided to take a trip to South Georgia with my mother and father. I figured I could use the get-away for my peace of mind and to help me get used to my new single life.

While in Georgia, my cousin Johnathan and I decided to go hang out and catch up. Johnathan's mom and my mom were sisters. He too was raised in a two-parent household.

We chose a popular, local, nightclub to visit. We found a spot in the back and ordered some drinks. The band didn't start until later, so we had some time to catch up before it would be too loud to talk.

"So, what have you been doing with yourself," I asked.

"Trying to do what my parents taught me," Johnathan laughed. "But it ain't easy being so fine."

We laughed.

Johnathan was tall, and indeed he was a very handsome, well-built man. He had style, and you could tell from how neat of a dresser he was that he cared about his appearance.

While we were catching up, this *dream* walked up to our table and spoke to my cousin.

"Johnathan," he said while looking at me. "Who is *this* lovely lady?"

I blushed, and Johnathan rolled his eyes.

"Michael, this is Jessica." He replied. "She's my cousin from Florida."

"What???" Michael stepped back and did a double take. "Little quiet, shy Jessica with the big eyes?"

I blushed from remembering how horrible I used to look as a kid.

"Milk has done your body good," Michael continued and smiled appreciatively.

I smiled widely. I remembered him now too from the times my family and I visited Georgia. He and Johnathan were good friends. They had both grown up in South Georgia. Milk had done him good too! Michael went to get us a round of drinks, and I quickly turned to Johnathan for the info.

"So, tell me about Michael," I said with wide eyes.

"He alright," Johnathan said rolling his eyes again. He was like a big brother being too protective. "But he *does* like the ladies and the ladies like him. Since his grandmother died, he been running wild."

Michael was handsome, so I understood why he was so popular. He was very close with his grandmother and Johnathan said he was hurt by her passing.

I hung out with Michael for the remainder of my Georgia visit and on the last day of my visit, I found leaving to be bittersweet because of my wonderful new friendship with Michael. We made a vow to keep in touch.

Back in Florida, I resumed my normal routine of work and school, but not a day went by that I didn't talk to Michael, sometimes for hours at a time. After a few months, I traveled back to Georgia with the sole purpose of visiting Michael.

This visit was different. He introduced me to his family and friends. It was during this visit that we decided to make our relationship official. We were in a long-distance relationship for a year before I decided to make a move to Georgia.

I took a risk on love and resigned from my job and transferred to the local college in South Georgia. I'd still be able to graduate on time, so it worked out perfectly.

The graduation ceremony was held in Florida, and all of my family were in attendance, and so was Michael. I was the first of my siblings to receive a College degree. I felt extremely accomplished.

Michael and I returned home to South Georgia, and a few months later I gained employment with a State of Georgia Organization. I soon found out that working for that organization and being a new Georgia resident had been a blessing. I didn't get the job because of who I knew; I got it based on my hard work and skills.

Unfortunately, it only took a year for me to realize that my goals and dreams were bigger than what that small town had to offer. So, Michael and I decided to relocate to Atlanta. Michael had previously lived in Atlanta and had no problem finding employment.

When I arrived in Atlanta, I was unemployed, but Michael had a job as a truck driver. We moved into a beautiful split-level home but had little to no furniture. Although I had no job, just being in Atlanta was the best feeling ever. I'm not sure if it's because my roots were from Georgia or what, but I had always wanted to live in Atlanta.

Over the next several months I applied for jobs all over the city and soon gained employment with a very well-known established company. My salary was the highest I had ever made, and I was ecstatic. The move seemed to be the best decision as far as my career was concerned, but not such a wise choice for my personal life.

It turns out Michael struggled with a hot temper and anger issues. And to make matters worse, his dysfunctional family (who had always hindered his growth and life) were now intruding in our relationship.

I felt like this was Deja Vue.

My First Child

TWO YEARS PASSED, and I became pregnant with my first child. I was in a state of shock.

I was employed full-time and had just started school at a well-known University to obtain my BA in Human Resource Management. I was enrolled in the Accelerated Degree program which consisted of completing a semester amount of work in eight weeks. So being pregnant seriously weighted down my already heavy plate. But I was more determined and focused than I had ever been. I worked and attended school the entire time I was pregnant.

As time passed, I came to enjoy being pregnant.

When I found out I was having a girl, I became even more than excited. I was going to have a little *mini-me*. Yes!!!!!

I must admit I had a great pregnancy. There were no complications, and I followed all my doctor's orders. Michael and I were both super excited about our soon-to-arrive bundle of joy.

He decided to make his part-time profession as a professional painter/home repairs, etc. his full-time occupation so he would be home every day with the baby and me.

"I think we should paint the baby's room yellow," I said. "Everyone has a pink room for their little girls."

"I think yellow is stupid," Michael said roughly. "Who cares what everyone else has. She's a girl and girls like pink."

"Not every girl likes pink," I said with hurt feelings. "I didn't."

"Well, you're definitely not every girl," he said.

I didn't know what he meant by that, but I was too tired and emotional to fight with him. Besides, I really didn't care what color he painted the room. As long as we had a healthy baby, I would be satisfied.

Although, our relationship wasn't perfect my pregnancy was at the forefront of any disagreements or arguments we had. Which is why I generally chose to give in, and we kept it moving.

When my ninth month finally arrived, I was ready and scared at the same time.

"I'm so happy," I said to Michael.

We were at the hospital, and I was about to become a mom. I had no idea what I was doing or how I was going to balance school, work, and now motherhood. But more than that, I was ready to meet my little girl.

I delivered my beautiful, healthy baby via C-section. This was the proudest day of my entire life.

Words cannot express the joy motherhood brought into my life. Everything in my life seemed to be falling into place.

The choice to become a mom was one choice I have never regretted.

The House Guest

ABOUT THREE MONTHS into our new life as parents, Michael approaches me with the most insane idea.

"Dad's gonna be released soon, and I want him to come live with us."

"Absolutely not," I said without hesitation. "We just had a baby."

"I know we have a baby," Michael said now angry. "But he's my father, and I think we should help him."

"Who is gonna help us," I said. "We have enough responsibilities."

"We don't have to care for him Jessica," Michael spat. "He just needs a place to stay until he gets on his feet."

I was *totally* against this for several reasons. Michael's father wasn't a part of his life growing up so why did he feel the need to take care of a man who hadn't taken care of him. Also, we were just starting to build a life together. We had a new home and a new baby; we simply didn't need any extra responsibilities.

After about a month or so of standing my ground and being labeled as *the bad person* by a few of Michael's family members, I made the choice to accept his proposal and finally gave in. "I don't care," I shouted. "Do whatever you want."

And so, within the next couple of months, Michael's father was released from Federal Prison and came to live with us.

Joe was a very handsome man. He was a true lady's man and preferred them young (and legal). He didn't look his age, so women of all ages fell for him. He had style and was very loyal but to the wrong friends. Michael used to say his father was a 'rolling stone.' After meeting him, I understood.

Joe was a charmer.

He had served a fifteen-year sentence. Although, I wasn't happy with this decision I put my feelings on the back-burner and went with the flow.

Over the next few weeks, Michael spent time getting his father familiar with living life from behind bars. It really amazed me how the little everyday things we take for granted was something that Michael's father had to learn and get accustomed to again.

For example, being in crowds at the mall, driving, and just being free to do what you want without being told were some of the things Joe struggled with.

One thing that I did grow to love about Michael's father was his cleanliness. Joe was just as neat and clean as I was when it came to keeping house. I found out that was also due to his prison time. They ran a tight ship in prison. You had to clean up behind yourself.

As time passed, Michael, me, our daughter and Joe adjusted to living as one big happy family. Believe it or not, things seemed to be working out better than I ever imagined. We all worked 9 to 5 jobs with weekends off.

Looking back, I guess Michael was so insistent on his father living with us because he didn't meet him until he was fifteen years old. Joe hadn't been a permanent part of his son's life. It was something Michael had craved, a father/son bond. So, naturally, when the opportunity presented itself, Michael jumped on it, perhaps hoping it would result in the type of relationship he'd wanted growing up.

I came to understand it, and the only thing that was truly bothersome for me during this time period was we often had random visitors stopping by to see Joe. I'm a people person, but I'm a private person primarily.

Of course, I voiced my feelings to Michael about this, but it only led to arguments.

"Who are all these people that keep coming over here, Michael?"

"How am I supposed to know, Jessica?" Michael would respond with annoyance. "Joe has a life outside of us and *he* is friendly. People like *him*."

The way he said it made me think he was accusing me of not being friendly or liked.

"What does *that* mean? Are you saying that *I'm* not a friendly person?" I asked and felt hurt. Michael was supposed to know me better than anyone.

"Well, I don't see anyone coming around here to see *you*," Michael pointed out. "Maybe *you're* just jealous."

"If I wanted friends, I could have them." I shouted. "I just don't want any drama. Besides, working and taking care of *our* child is *my* primary responsibility."

Things got so bad that a few times I even attempted to leave Michael. His bad temper, the anger issues, his lack of emotional support, and putting his family's needs and wants before mine were too much to bear.

But each time he convinced me things would get better and so I always made the choice to stay.

Chaos

A YEAR AFTER JOE came to live with us something disturbing happened.

"I've been getting calls from the DEA," Michael said out of the blue.

"What?" I asked totally confused. "Why?"

"They are asking me questions about my father."

"What kinds of questions," I asked. "And why are they talking to *you* instead of to Joe?"

"I don't know Jessica," Michael responded with irritation. "They were asking me about Dad's friend Henry. What the hell do I know about Henry? They were talking to me like I was a kid, so I hung up on them."

I was in total shock because I was raised to respect law enforcement. I was so upset with Michael for handling things as he did.

"Michael, it's not a good idea to talk to them that way, and you certainly can't hang up in their faces!"

"Why the hell not," Michael shouted. "Are you on their side or mine?"

"That's a stupid question," I said. "I'm on your side, but I don't want you to get into any trouble over this."

The argument got heated, and finally, Michael ended it by saying, "Jessica, why can't you just let a man be a man? I will handle this!"

I took a deep breath in and exhaled. Then I said, "Ok MAN. Handle it."

I walked away from that conversation and made the choice that I *would not* interfere and *did not* want to know *anything* about what was going on.

But I did warn him.

"If shit hits the fan, DO NOT seek *my* help," I said sarcastically. "Just handle it like a MAN."

I had never been in any trouble with the law. Therefore, I didn't know how these types of situations worked.

Other than a few misdemeanor arrests, Michael had never been in any major trouble with the law either, so he really wasn't educated to how things concerning DEA agents worked either.

Although he was a bit more educated with the law than me, neither of us would have ever guessed how our lives would be turned upside down and left in total chaos in the next coming months.

Headline News

THE MORNING STARTED out as any typical Monday. I got myself ready for work and my daughter to be handed off to the sitter. It was still dark outside as I carried my daughter out to the car. As I leaned inside preparing to strap my daughter into her car seat, I heard sirens and saw flashing red lights.

The rest occurred so fast; I could hardly comprehend what was happening.

"Where is Michael?" The male agent shouted at me while a female agent pushed her way to my daughter and me.

"He's inside," I cried. "What's going on?"

Then I heard, "Put your hands up and get down on the ground!"

I followed the direction of the voices and realized they were pointing guns toward the door of my home.

Then Michael appeared.

He was standing there in only his boxers, looking confused and very angry. When he finally realized it wasn't a dream, he complied with the officer's commands and put both of his hands up in the air and then laid down on the ground.

The team of officers swarmed in on him with their guns raised and handcuffed him.

Of course, I'm in a complete state of shock. I'm holding on to my daughter so tight; she begins to squirm. She was only 23 months old and didn't understand what was going on. I didn't understand what was going on.

Michael was handcuffed and on the ground. Then things went from bad to worse.

"Ma'am, you're under arrest," the female agent said to me as she took my daughter from my arms.

The male agent handcuffed me, and I lost it.

"What did I do," I cried hysterically. "What is going on?"

"I'm going to need you to calm down ma'am," the female agent said softly. "You're upsetting your daughter."

It took a minute for what she was saying to register with me because all I could think about was that I hadn't done anything wrong, they were handcuffing me, and a stranger was now holding my child. It was too much to process.

But Morgan was amazing.

She didn't cry or seem upset. She looked around at all the officers and commotion and then stared at me. I'm sure she was just as confused as I was, maybe even in shock. She definitely handled it better than her dad and me.

By this time our neighbors began to notice something was going on. They were looking out their windows, and some even came outside. School kids were walking to their bus stop, and it seemed everyone had their eyes on us. Our driveway became headline news.

One of the officers noticed the attention we were getting and told his counterparts to escort us (myself, Michael, and the agent holding Morgan) to the inside of our home.

Once inside, things began to make sense.

"Where's Joe?" The agent asked.

"He's at work," Michael responded.

"Call him," the agent said. "Tell him he needs to get here now."

They took my handcuffs off (I guess I was considered less of a threat than Michael) so I could call Joe from my cell phone.

"Joe," I said as calmly as I could. "You need to get home now.

I'm sure Joe could hear the distress in my voice. "What's -"

"I can't explain now," I said cutting him off. "You just need to get here as fast as you can."

The agent took the phone from me and ended the call and informed me of another call I needed to make.

"I need you to call someone to come get your daughter," the female officer said to me. "Otherwise, we will have to release her into DFACS custody."

I lost it again. Michael and I were going to jail, and so was Joe. And my sweet baby was going to be placed into the custody of the state. What was going on?! I needed answers, but they were going to have to wait.

"Stop crying Jessica," Michael ordered from across the room. Even though he was handcuffed, he somehow felt he could control things. "Call Mrs. Thomas."

My parents were in two different states (Florida and North Carolina) at the time, so I thank God for Mrs. Thomas. She had been classmates with my parents and Michael's mom too. She was sweet, loving, caring, thoughtful and kind. She treated Morgan as if she were her own child. I calmed down long enough to do what Michael said. I took a deep breath and made the call to our daughter's sitter.

"Mrs. Thomas," I said slowly. "I need you to come get Morgan this morning."

I know she knew something was terribly wrong, but she didn't ask any questions.

"I'm on my way," she said instead. And I hung up the phone.

Within no time, she arrived, and I began to feel a sense of relief. In the midst of this mess, I at least knew that our daughter would be safe. Mrs. Thomas would take great care of Morgan.

Although shocked and confused, Mrs. Thomas gathered Morgan and a few of her things and headed for the front door. Just as she was about to step outside, Morgan began to cry.

I looked to the female officer for approval to go to my daughter. She nodded, and I ran to my baby and hugged her while she was in Mrs. Thomas arms.

"It's ok baby,'" I said even though I knew it wasn't. "You're going to be fine with Mrs. Thomas. I love you."

I hugged her tight and then I whispered in Mrs. Thomas ear, "Take care of my baby. As soon as I find out what's going on, I'll call you."

Mrs. Thomas nodded and then left with my baby.

Shoulders Back

AGENT SMITH, the agent in charge, was tall and heavyset. He showed me a piece of paper with a list of names on it; mine was the last one on the list.

"I'm going to need you to sign this paper, so we can search your residence." His voice was menacing and filled with arrogance.

"Is this a search warrant?" I asked.

"No," he replied smugly. Clearly, he was used to being in charge and getting what he wanted at all costs.

"Then I'm not signing it," I said firmly. I didn't know what was going on, but I'd watched enough crime shows to know that I had some rights.

I don't think Agent Smith was happy about that and he made sure I knew it.

To add insult to injury, and even though he didn't have a search warrant and never presented any type of legal document, Agent Smith looked at me and shouted to one of the officers, "Call the tow company and have them pick up their cars."

His tone was nasty, and the intent was received. We were in for a fight.

The shock was wearing off, and I knew that I had to show some sense of confidence or I'd be railroaded into confessing to something I didn't do. I'd seen that on crime show TV too. So, I wiped my tears and sat up straight.

"Can I phone my job?" I asked with a voice I didn't recognize. "I need to let them know I won't be in today."

To my surprise, he agreed to it and also allowed me to call my parents.

The call to my job was quick and done with ease. However, calling my parents was a different story. I hadn't been raised this way. I had no frame of reference for this life or how to live it. I didn't want to upset my parents, but I knew they needed to hear news like this from me and not from anyone else.

"Mom," I said, desperately trying to keep my emotions in check. "This is Jessica. Michael and I are being arrested, and Morgan is with Mrs. Thomas."

I had to pull the phone back from my ear. Mom began crying instantly and simultaneously asking me more questions than I'd ever be able to answer.

"Mom," I shouted into the phone. "I can't go into details right now, but I need you to tell Dad. I need you to check in with Mrs. Thomas. And I need you to be strong and pray for us."

I looked at Michael, and he had this defiant look on his face. In my mind, this was all his fault. If he had never allowed Joe to come live with us, none of this would be happening. I knew it.

But the look on Michael's face told me he didn't feel that way.

I didn't have an ally here in this room. So, I knew I had to be strong so that I could survive this.

I hung up the phone and shortly thereafter, Joe arrived. He was immediately placed under arrest. I found it surprising that unlike us, Joe had been down this road before, and yet he seemed just as shocked and in utter disbelief as we were.

He complied with the officer's request and didn't say anything. He also didn't answer any of their questions.

Michael was allowed to get dressed, I was re-cuffed, and the three of us were loaded into a transport van and taken to an undisclosed location in downtown Atlanta.

Inside, I was falling apart. But on the outside, I held my head high and kept my shoulders back. All I could think about was seeing Morgan again.

A Sickening Feeling

WE WERE HELD for several hours, but still, none of the authorities would tell us why we were being detained. We had no idea what was going on.

Joe and Michael quickly realized that the agents did not have a search or arrest warrant when they came into our home.

We later learned this was why we were being held in an undisclosed location while they went before a judge to obtain the warrants.

The morning's chaos had us in such a state that we failed to realize that in addition to there not being any warrants, we were also never read our rights.

The only thing that was presented to me was that plain piece of paper with our names listed on it. That was also the paper they tried to get me to sign, but which I had refused.

Finally, after several hours of waiting, the signed arrest warrants materialized, and we were officially booked.

The booking process was the most horrific and humiliating process any human being could ever be subjected to.

I was told that my charge was drug conspiracy. I was fingerprinted and then my mugshot was taken.

With every step of the process, I found myself becoming numb inside. It was like I was having an out-of-body mental experience.

Next, I was escorted to a holding cell that was filled with lots of other women. On the way to the women's holding cell, we passed by the holding cell for men and of course I had to endure the whistling and the 'hey baby' catcalls and tons of other ignorant things those men were shouting out to me. It was like walking the green mile. I had a sickening feeling in my stomach that I prayed wouldn't stay with me forever.

It was now lunchtime, and the jail staff began handing out lunch.

"Jessica," I heard Michael yell. "Make sure you eat because I don't know how long it will be before they serve the next meal."

Eating was the last thing on my mind. I was too distraught. I didn't listen and gave my lunch away to one of the other women in the cell.

I will starve to death before I eat a crumb of what they serve me here, I thought.

Mind Over Matter

THE MORE TIME went by, the emptier I felt inside.

Around 5 pm, I found out that I could bond out on a signature bond. That meant all I had to do was sign a piece of paper and abide by whatever stipulations the bond came with (I was considered low risk since I had no prior record, so my only stipulation was that I not get into any trouble.).

By 6 pm, I was released. It was cold and dark outside. The jail staff allowed me to use their phone, so I called Mrs. Thomas.

"Hello," I said. "Mrs. Thomas, It's Jessica. I'm being released, and I was wondering if you could come pick me up."

Mrs. Thomas was elderly and not a fan of driving at night in the crazy Atlanta downtown traffic but assured me she'd muster up enough courage to come. She made me promise to be outside and on the corner near the traffic light, so she wouldn't have to try to find parking.

I stood outside in the freezing cold for nearly 45 minutes before Mrs. Thomas, and my daughter finally arrived.

I was so happy to see them both. I cried the entire ride home as I tried to explain to Mrs. Thomas what had happened to me.

She dropped Morgan and me off and told me to call her if we needed anything.

Once inside, I hugged Morgan tight. She laid her pretty little head on my shoulder, and I thanked God for letting me see her again. I didn't let her see my tears, but I was crying like I was the baby.

Finally, I got us both ready for bed. I was mentally and physically exhausted. I managed to call my parents to let them know I was home and then Morgan and I drifted off to sleep.

The next morning was Friday, and I had to be at work. I got up and pushed myself to begin the day as I would any other day. As I dressed, I kept saying to myself; *you are stronger than your circumstances* and *mind over matter.*

I know it was the God-given strength that filled my soul with that 'get up and fight, don't give up' attitude. I was hurt, confused, embarrassed and so much more at what had taken place. Yet I knew I had to go on.

I didn't know the details, but what I did know was that I was innocent of any wrongdoing and my rights had been violated.

I am my father's child, violate our rights and our *stand up and fight* kicks in. My father is a man who believes in fairness and equal/just treatment for all. When we feel those rights have been violated, its only natural for us to fight to make it right.

Thankfully they hadn't impounded Michael's father's car because that was the only transportation I had. So, I was able to drop Morgan off at Mrs. Thomas and make my way to work.

No one noticed anything different about me which in my mind was a good thing. I hadn't planned on telling anyone that I'd just experienced hell on earth.

The fact that they couldn't see my inner turmoil meant I was wearing it (strength, faith) well.

Well as far as they could see I was strong. I admit to having several mini breakdowns throughout the day.

I would find myself crying in the bathroom stall and wishing I could flush my troubles down the drain.

My workday finally came to an end.

Although my whole world had changed in a matter of minutes, by the grace of God, I was able to make it through the day without anyone noticing anything different about me.

Remember, You're Innocent

I LEFT WORK and headed to Mrs. Thomas to pick up Morgan. On the way, I received a collect phone call from jail.

It was Michael.

"How are you?" He asked. "How is Morgan?"

"Under the circumstances, we are ok."

"I'm trying to get a bond, but they giving me the run-around on purpose. That DEA guy has a personal vendetta against me."

"Well, I guess he didn't like the way you spoke to him when he initially called you," I said sarcastically.

"Whatever Jessica," Michael said sounding weary. "Now is not the time for that. Anyway, they are not giving Joe bail. He's already on parole, so this doesn't look good for him."

I had a hard time feeling sorry for either of them. Whatever they had done, I knew I hadn't been a part of it, yet I was in just as deep as they were. I thought about my choice NOT to ask questions when I should have and wondered if that had been a grave mistake.

"I'll call you back when I find out more," Michael said.

"Ok," I replied dryly and hung up the phone. I worked hard to keep the tears inside. I couldn't afford to get weak now.

I finally arrived at Mrs. Thomas to pick up Morgan. Seeing my baby's smiling face reminded me that I had to remain strong through this ordeal. She needed me.

As I drove home, I silently thanked God that tomorrow was Saturday and that I didn't work on weekends. I needed some time to gather my thoughts and begin to put together a plan for what I'd do next.

The next morning, I woke up and decide to check my mail. There was a letter for me from the Georgia Federal Court. The letter was in reference to my arraignment hearing which had been scheduled to take place in two weeks.

I had no idea what an arraignment hearing was but soon found out after I did a little research.

An arraignment was a formal reading of a criminal charging document in the presence of the defendant to inform the defendant of the charges against them. In response to arraignment, the defendant is expected to enter a plea.

Receiving this letter only reminded me of just how serious this situation was. I immediately phoned my mother.

"Ma, I'm in trouble," I cried. "I got a letter in the mail from the court. They are charging me, Mama!"

"Calm down Jessica," she said. "Remember you're innocent. This is all a misunderstanding. All you've got to do is hang in there while they figure this mess out."

"Yes ma'am," I said, and I did feel a glimmer of hope. She was right. I hadn't done anything, so they'd figure it out soon enough, and all of this would go away for me.

"I'll come and stay with you and Morgan for a few weeks and that way I can attend the arraignment hearing with you too."

I nodded my head and felt somewhat better.

"I love you, Mama," I said and wiped the tears from my face. "Thank you for being so supportive. I'll see you soon."

"Bye bye baby."

After hanging up the phone, I spent the remainder of my weekend loving on Morgan and contemplating if I needed to hire an attorney or not. Even though I wasn't guilty of anything, I didn't want to be under-represented.

Monday morning came quickly, and it was time to start the week all over again. As I was driving Morgan to the sitter, I received another collect call from the jail. It was Michael again.

"Hey baby," he said. "How are you and Morgan?"

"We're still doing fine," I said. Actually, I think I was numb and operating in automatic pilot mode. This all still seemed so unreal.

I couldn't believe it was happening.

"Now they saying they lost my paperwork during the intake process," Michael said clearly upset. "This is starting to really piss me off."

I had to agree with him. Something wasn't adding up. I told him about the arraignment papers I got in the mail.

"Yea, me and Joe got some too," he said.

"I don't know if I need to get an attorney or not," I said.

He gave me the name of an attorney to contact. A fellow inmate had given him the information.

"Call her," Michael said. "She can give you feedback or advice about what you need to do."

"What will you do about getting an attorney for yourself?"

"I don't know Jessica," Michael sighed. "Right now, I'm focused on you and making sure you get your name cleared. I'll ask about an attorney for me later."

We hung up, and I immediately contacted Attorney Vile, at Michael's suggestion. I gave her the short version of what happened the day the agents came to our home and what I was being charged with.

"The charges against will you probably be dropped," Attorney Vile stated. "You'll be assigned a Public Defender at the arraignment hearing. I suggest you attend that arraignment with your Public Defender."

I nodded my head and then remembered she couldn't see me. This whole ordeal was making me crazy. "Yes ma'am," I finally said into the phone.

"After the arraignment, if you still find that you need to hire me," she said. "Give me a call then."

Culpable

LATER THAT DAY, Michael called back, and I told him what I'd found out from Attorney Vile. He was relieved to hear that Attorney Vile felt that the charges against me would be dropped.

He was still being told that his paperwork was lost and until they were found, he couldn't bond out. He said he was going to have to hire an attorney because that would be the only way he was going to get his bond processed.

Michael's plan was similar to mine, to attend the Arraignment Hearing using his assigned Public Defender and once that was over, ask his mom to hire him a private attorney. The only difference is I was sure I wouldn't need to hire an attorney after my arraignment. They would see that I was innocent.

My mother arrived in town the next week, and it was now two days away from the arraignment hearing.

I continued to work every day, and instead of going to the sitter's, Morgan stayed with my mother.

Although my mother didn't really understand to the full extent of what was going on, she supported me completely. She was there for me emotionally and did anything she could do financially in terms of helping me with groceries, gas money, and anything Morgan needed, etc.

Finally, the day of the arraignment hearing arrived, and my mother accompanied me. We dropped Morgan off at Ms. Thomas and drove 2 ½ hours away to South Georgia.

Although we lived in Atlanta (North GA), the case was out of the Southern District of Georgia.

I was an emotional wreck the entire drive and tried not to show it to my mother, but a mother knows.

Although I had printed the google map directions (I didn't have a phone with GPS at that time), I got lost once we got into the downtown area and had to stop and ask an officer for directions.

We finally found the courthouse.

There were 38 people on the case, and all of us were in attendance. Of that number, thirty-four (including Joe) took plea deals and opted not to go to trial.

The remaining four (me, Michael, Michael's friend and one other person) entered not guilty pleas and chose to go to trial.

The first time I met or even saw my Public Defender was when the judge called me up to enter my plea of 'Not Guilty."

We were told that we would be notified of a trial date.

On the way out of the courtroom Mr. Smith (my Public Defender) leans over and whispers to me with an evil laugh, "They tell me you are the least culpable one here and if you cooperate, we can get you out of this mess."

I didn't say one word.

I knew I wasn't guilty. I just gave him a look and thought to myself; *I will be hiring Ms. Vile to represent me.*

The Cards We're Dealt

MY MOTHER AND I traveled the 2 ½ hour drive back home to North Georgia without really saying much. We both were in a state of disbelief. One thing we both agreed on was that we thought the charges against me would be dropped.

Mom decided she would stay with Morgan and me for another week before heading back home.

The next day I contacted Attorney Vile and told her what happened at the arraignment hearing. She was totally shocked and agreed to represent me.

My father paid the retainer fee (for which I was so grateful), and now I felt prepared to fight; I was armed with a hired attorney instead of a court-appointed one. But even with that sense of security, the whole situation was still so unsettling to me.

Later on that day Attorney Vile contacted me on my cell phone while I was at work.

"Hello Jessica, this is Attorney Vile. I wanted to bring you up to date on where we are so far."

I was nervous. The butterflies in my stomach had been fluttering nonstop. I wasn't sure what she was going to say, so I nodded my head and waited for her to continue.

"I spoke with the District Attorney regarding your case and your specific involvement. It all boils down to the fact that you are Michael's girlfriend. The DEA agents and the District Attorney are truly upset at Michael and how he disrespected them when they initially tried to contact him, and now it appears they have a vendetta to settle."

I exhaled. I knew I was innocent, but I also knew that I didn't want to be an enemy of the courts – even by association.

I thanked Attorney Vile for the update and quickly ended the call.

Later that day when Michael called, I recalled the events of the day.

"Hey baby, how are you holding up?"

"As best I can," I responded. I was so tired; I could barely muster up enough strength to feel anything. The only thing that kept me going was Morgan. I had to be there for my baby. "I hired that attorney today, Ms. Vile."

"That was probably a good idea," Michael agreed. "My mom is going to hire me one too because waiting on the 'so-called' lost paperwork, so I can bond out of jail is going nowhere quick. And I found out those @$%^ have been to my mom's house, harassing her with questions and threatening to arrest her if she doesn't cooperate."

I was silent. It hadn't occurred to me that they would go after our family members too. I was now afraid for my parents.

Michael told me he instructed his mother to invoke her 5th amendment rights if the DEA stop by her house again.

We talked about Attorney Vile and then about nothing. Our already strained relationship was crumbling under the weight of this latest blow. I wasn't sure it would withstand the test.

Later in the week, I got another call from Attorney Vile while I was at work. She didn't sound like herself, and right away I was worried.

"Jessica," she began with a sternness to her voice that hadn't been there earlier. "You *really* need to cooperate with the authorities, or this is not going to end well for you."

"I have been cooperating," I said now defensive. "I don't have answers for the questions they are asking me."

"The authorities want you to come and answer questions about Michael. I'll be there with you this time. You won't have nothing to worry about."

Hell immediately flew in me, and I lost my composure. "I HAVE NOTHING TO DO WITH

WHAT'S GOING ON, AND I WANT MY NAME OUT OF THIS MESS," I told her. "I hired *you* to represent me because I felt my appointed Public Defender couldn't be trusted and *now* you are making me wonder if I can trust you. You represent *me*, not Michael. I want my name cleared!"

I could tell Attorney Vile was shocked by my response and more than a little angry with me.

"I'll be in contact," she said shortly and ended the call.

That phone call upset me so much; I couldn't continue to work. I immediately went to the restroom to calm myself. Once inside the restroom stall, I cried my eyes out, and my thoughts and emotions were all over the place.

Finally, I said a prayer, got myself together and returned to my office and carried on with the workday.

During my lunch, I was hoping to hear from Michael. I needed to know what was going on. I only had ten minutes left in my lunch break when my phone rang. It was Michael.

"Hey baby," he said and right away I knew something was wrong.

"What's wrong?" I asked, but unsure I really wanted to know.

"They came and arrested my mother today."

I was in a state of shock. "What? Why? How can they do this and get away with it!!!!"

"Jessica, baby, please calm down," We'll get through this somehow. I know you gotta get back to work. As soon as I find out more, I'll let you know."

We ended the call, and I returned to my office with a heavy heart and weary mind. But as usual, I was able to push through my workday without anyone noticing how upset I was from that phone call.

I filled my thoughts with making it through the day, so I could see, hold, and kiss my baby girl. Those thoughts always helped soothe my mind. I focused on her instead of the chaos which was quickly consuming my life.

On the drive home, my phone rings; it's Michael.

"Mom's been released on a signature bond," he said. "But she is now a part of this mess and being charged with drug conspiracy just like we are. And now they are transferring me to the county jail in South Georgia because the case (indictment) is out of that District."

My mind was whirling with so much negative information. I just held the phone and listened as Michael told me he felt these latest antics were just more of the same, vindictive tactics the DEA was using to make things more chaotic for him because of the racial slurs he spewed at them when they initially tried to contact him. Now he was being labeled as extremely uncooperative.

Within the next couple of days, Michael was transferred to a jail in South Georgia.

His mother hired him a private attorney (recommended by a guy he met in jail). Her name was Attorney Glenda Jackson. Attorney Jackson was short, stout, and plain. The day after she was officially hired, she was able to get Michael into court for a bond hearing.

The DEA agents and the District Attorney did everything in their power to make it difficult for Michael to be granted a bond, including telling the judge that Michael threatened them when they initially contacted him and that he was a flight risk (among other things).

All were failed attempts because according to the law Michael was due a bond even though he let his temper get the best of him initially.

The judge finally granted Michael's bond, but it entailed a couple of huge stipulations:

He couldn't return home to Atlanta to live with our daughter and me.

He also couldn't operate his business.

This meant he had to live in South Georgia with his mom until the case went to trial.

Attorney Jackson tried her best to get the judge to disagree with these stipulations, but the judge wouldn't budge, and the stipulations remained intact.

Although he was getting out of jail, Michael would still be separated from his family and his livelihood. In some form, he was still incarcerated.

Michael's release was good news, but the stipulation of him living with his mother and not with us only added insult to injury.

It took me some time to come to terms with the judge's decision, but I was determined not to let it beat me down. So, I came up with a plan.

My daughter and I would drive to South Georgia (2 ½ to 3 hours away from Atlanta) twice a month (Saturdays and Sundays and sometimes leaving Fridays after work) to spend family time with Michael.

I decided we would spend holidays with him too.

My attitude was to remain as positive as possible and play the cards we were being dealt.

Praying My Way Through

IT WAS MONDAY, which meant work for me and the babysitter for Morgan. The day was going pretty good under the circumstances until I received a call from Attorney Vile. Once again, the call was full of threats of what would happen to me if I didn't agree to meet with DEA agents to answer questions about Michael.

And just like before, I had to remind Attorney Vile of what her job was.

"As I said before," I began heatedly. "What I need you to do is focus on clearing *my* name. You're *my* attorney, not Michael's. I'm beginning to wonder if I can trust you. I already don't trust the DEA. Not once have you called me to discuss the evidence they supposedly have against me or my involvement in this mess. Instead, your calls are scare tactics. You're trying to bully me into meeting with the DEA agents."

I was on a roll and very upset. Attorney Vile wasn't saying anything, so I continued. "Do not call me anymore with threats or ask me to meet with any law enforcement officials."

I ended the call and made my way to what was becoming a normal hang out for me – the work bathroom.

Silently, I cried my eyes out. I thought hiring a private attorney would work in my favor, but Attorney Vile was proof that I was wrong.

I pulled myself together enough to say a prayer before I exited the restroom. I was able to make it through the rest of my workday productively in-spite of my restroom stall breakdown.

During my drive from work, Michael called, and I told him all about Attorney Vile's upsetting phone call. Of course, he lost it and began to spew out all kinds of profanities, and I co-signed every one of them.

Michael did end our phone conversation with some good news. He told me that although he hadn't found permanent work yet, he had secured three house painting jobs, which was great news considering he now had no income since the judge forbade him from operating his own business.

I ended the call with Michael as I arrived at the sitter to pick-up Morgan.

We finally arrived home, and I checked the mail before going inside. To my surprise, there were two letters from a local Atlanta tow yard. I opened one of the letters and nearly passed out.

According to the letter, my Toyota Avalon (which had been sitting at their tow yard for over 30 days) had accumulated a fee of $1500. I opened the second letter and was hit with another shocker,

Michael's GMC Yukon (which had also been sitting at their tow yard for over 30 days) had also accumulated a fee of $1500.

All this time I had been under the impression that the DEA agents had our cars towed to some type of holding facility that they used. The letters listed a number for me to call for further instructions.

I followed the letter's instructions and spoke with a guy named Tony. Tony told me that I had to call Agent Smith in order to have my vehicles released and gave me Agent Smith's contact information.

"Will you work with me on paying these fees," I asked Tony. I'm sure he could hear the weariness in my voice. "I had no idea that our vehicles were towed from our residence to your tow yard."

"I tell you what," Tony relented to my surprise. "If you can bring me $1500 in two days, I'll release both vehicles to you and won't charge you any further fees."

Although $1500 was still a lot of money, it was considerably less than $3000, so I thanked Tony and told him I would be in touch.

I immediately called Agent Smith and told him I received the letters from the tow yard and asked would he kindly call Tony at the tow yard and have my vehicles released.

"Yes," Agent Smith said. "I will make the call. You know Jessica, all you have to do is come talk to me and you can get yourself out of all this mess."

"I have to consult with my attorney," I said. I wasn't about to fall for any tricks.

I ended the call with Agent Smith, sat back on the couch and allowed myself to think about my newest worry.

Now, where in the hell am I going to get $1500.00?

I Didn't Know My Own Strength

I PHONED MY FATHER and told him about the situation with my vehicles. He didn't hesitate to ask how much I needed. I told him $1500, and although he was frustrated and couldn't understand why law enforcement was using such illegal tactics, he quickly said, "I'll put it in your bank account tomorrow."

I thanked my father and ended the call.

Now I had to figure out who could I get to help me pick up my vehicles. Then all of a sudden it came to me, my cousin Johnathan; the cousin I hung out with in South Georgia while vacationing with my parents when I met Michael.

After getting Johnathan to agree to help me, I phoned Tony at the tow yard and told him I would be there the next day with payment to pick up both vehicles.

The next morning, I contacted my job and informed them that I wouldn't be in due to a personal matter. I took Morgan to the sitter and returned home to await Johnathan's arrival.

He finally arrived at my house, parked his car in my driveway and rode with me to the tow yard.

I'd been driving Joe's car since this whole thing started.

We made our way to the tow yard. I paid Tony and then Johnathan and I drove the vehicles back to my house. I left Joe's car there at the tow yard. Johnathan drove Michael's truck, and I drove my car back to my house. Then Johnathan got in his car and drove me back to the tow yard to pick up Joe's car.

I thanked Johnathan for his help, and finally headed home.

Once I got home, I sat on the couch and began to thank God for making a way out of no way once again.

Then I called Michael.

"Hey baby," I said cheerily. "I have some good news. Dad gave me the money to get our cars out of tow, and Johnathan helped me get them home."

Michael was relieved. "That's great news baby. Make sure you thank everyone for me."

My family wasn't too happy with Michael right now. He wasn't on their list of favorite people for obvious reasons, so I understood why he didn't call and thank them himself.

Michael and I conversed about our weekend plans which entailed Morgan and I making a trip down to South Georgia to see him and spend family time together.

"I can't wait to see you and baby girl," Michael said sounding more like himself than he had in weeks.

"I'm looking forward to it too," I said. "And so is Morgan."

"Have you thought about how you can get my truck down here to me," Michael asked. "It would make getting back and forth to work a lot easier if I had my own ride."

"I know," I said. "I'll figure something out."

We talked a bit more but decided we'd sleep on it and talk about it more the next day.

I ended the call with Michael and decided to relax until it was time to get Morgan from the babysitter.

The next day and I awoke with a bit more pep in my step. Finally, it looked like things were going my way. Finally, I would be driving my own car to work. I thanked God and was truly grateful for Joe's car, but there's nothing like your own!

I dropped Morgan off to the sitter as usual and headed to work. The day went well, and without any nasty, threating phone calls from Attorney Vile.

On the drive home, I spoke with Michael. He had come up with a plan for getting his truck to him. His cousin Albert was in Atlanta visiting a friend and would be leaving the same day that Morgan and I were and had agreed to drive Michael's truck.

More good news. The day ended on a high note.

The rest of the work week was as smooth as butter. And by Friday, I had been lulled into a sense of peace and hopefulness about the future. Somehow, I knew all of this mess would blow over, and Michael and I could go on with our lives before the nightmare began.

I was looking forward to the end of the day. I had plans to pack for Morgan and my first trip to South Georgia to visit Michael.

Saturday morning at 7:00 am, there was a knock at the door. It was Michael's cousin, Albert. Albert was tall, quiet and a southern gentleman.

"Where are your bags," Albert asked. "I"ll load them in the car for you."

"Already done," I said pleasantly. "We're all ready to go."

I had packed and loaded our bags into my car the night before therefore, there was nothing for Albert to do but get the keys to Michael's truck. We stopped for gas and then were well on our way. Albert trailed me the entire trip to Michael's mom's house.

Two and a half hours later, we arrived, and before I could get Morgan out of her car seat, Michael was standing behind me with a huge smile and welcoming arms.

Michael talked with Albert for a couple minutes and thanked him for his help. Albert's ride arrived shortly thereafter to pick him up and then myself, Michael and Morgan went inside to enjoy each other's company.

We talked, laughed and hugged on one another for a few hours and decided to go out for dinner.

The nicest restaurant in the area was located one county over from where Michael's mom lived. It didn't matter to us as long as we were together.

Dinner was nice, we didn't talk much about the pending criminal case and the havoc it was reaping in our lives. Michael was more concern with Morgan and my well-being and updated me on his job search and the handyman home repair jobs he was working until he obtained a permanent full-time job.

After dinner, it took us about 30 minutes to get back to Michael's mom's house. His mom, two brothers, niece, nephew, and his brother's wife were at the house when we arrived. The adults sat in the living room discussing the case while the kids went into the den to play.

Before we knew it, it was after midnight. We all said our goodnights and goodbyes and prepared for bed.

Sunday morning arrived much too soon. Before long, it was time for Morgan and me to return to Atlanta. I planned to leave around noon in order to have time to prepare for work. Michael insisted on making breakfast for us (something he would often do when we were in our own place), and it felt good to do something we were familiar with.

I got Morgan and myself dressed while Michael put our luggage in the car.

"Be safe baby," Michael said and pulled me into his arms.

I was trying not to cry in front of Morgan. I didn't want to upset my baby. I had to be strong.

"I will," I said holding back tears which made it hard to speak.

We had a great first visit, but it was extremely sad saying goodbye.

It wasn't until the drive back that the reality of the situation began to sink in. This was truly a traumatic experience.

I looked in my rearview mirror at Morgan.

I promise you baby girl; I will fight to keep our family together, I thought.

We arrived home, and I put Morgan down to play while I unpacked, made dinner and prepared for the upcoming week. I didn't get into bed that night until after 10 pm.

I was tired but somehow encouraged.

I was determined not to break.

The radio was playing and at that moment, I realized Whitney Houston was singing a line from what had become my theme song, "I was not built to break."

More Than A Conqueror

MONDAY MORNING was the beginning of a new week. I got dressed and prepared Morgan for the sitter, and we were off on our normal routine.

I had a "more than a conqueror" mindset and was actually being productive in my workload. I'd been assigned a few complicated tasks but was putting a dent in them.

Time passed quickly while I was working and so I was shocked when I looked down and saw it was noon, my lunchtime.

My phone rang, and it was Michael. He was upset.

"Baby, I feel like I would have been better off in jail. They got me tied down so tight; I can't move anyway!"

"What's wrong Michael?"

"I just got off the phone with Attorney Jackson," he began. "Now, I've been informed that on top of everything else, I have a curfew. I have to be home by 6 pm every night!"

My heart sank. We didn't need any more bad news. Just when I thought things were looking up. A curfew meant that when Morgan and I visited we wouldn't be able to go out for a dinner, movie or any other family activity that people did in the evenings.

It also meant that Michael had to make a big adjustment to his job search.

It was beginning to feel like the more we tried to make the most of this chaotic situation, the worse it got.

"I think they are watching us and tapping our phones," Michael went on to say. "That's how they found out about our family time. This new stipulation is just another way to break us."

I agreed with him. Every piece of happy or peace they saw us having, was what they seemed interested in taking.

"I don't know how much more of this I can take," I said quietly.

"I think we should get married," Michael said out of the blue. "That way you can't be made to testify against me once this thing does make it to court."

I didn't know what to feel. Every girl dreams of marriage, but not like this.

"I don't know Michael," I said cautiously.

"What is there to know?" He asked. "You love me don't you?"

"Well yes I do," I said. "But you never talked about marriage before all of this mess got started."

Michael was silent then. I didn't have anything further to add either, so we ended the call. I had to get back to work anyway, but before I did, I made my usual pitstop – the bathroom.

I stood quietly in the stall looking up at the ceiling as tears rolled down my cheeks. I thought to myself, *God, please help me.*

I returned to my desk and finished out my workday as if nothing happened. On my drive from work, Michael called again.

For a brief second, I thought about not answering his call. I had had enough for one day, but I pushed those feelings aside and took the call.

"I got a letter today about the evidentiary hearing."

"What is that," I asked. I was becoming more and more familiar with the judicial system. But I can't say I was proud of that.

"It's a hearing at which evidence is presented and heard by the court," Michael replied.

"Oh ok," I said simply. "I will check the mail when I get home to see if I have one too."

We ended the call, and I went on and picked up Morgan from the sitter. I checked my mail, but to my surprise, there was no mail in my box.

I phoned Michael to let him know and told him I would phone Attorney Vile tomorrow to inquire about my evidentiary letter.

As soon as I ended the call with Michael, my phone rings.

It was my cousin, Johnathan.

"Hey cousin, I'm in a bind," he said. "I need a place to stay for a while."

"I need to talk to Michael about that first," I said. "I'll let you know something tomorrow."

Even though Michael wasn't allowed to live here, this was still very much his home too. Johnathan was a single dad and had never been married. I knew how hard it was raising a child alone and really wanted to help him out. However, I wanted to respect Michael.

I ended the call with Johnathan, cooked a quick meal for Morgan and I and we ate. By the time we finished eating, it was time to prepare for bed.

The day had been long, and as far as I was concerned, it still wasn't over. I laid in bed thinking about the choices I had made in the past and decisions I had to make now.

Suddenly, I realized I wasn't confident in my abilities to make the right choices anymore.

Do I marry Michael?

Should I provide a temporary roof for my cousin?

How can I help someone else when my own life is in such turmoil?

The questions kept rolling in and needless to say, I didn't get much sleep, but the new day arrived anyway, and duty was calling. I put thoughts and feelings aside and pressed forward.

My plan was to spend my lunch break making a few important phones calls.

I needed to call Attorney Vile, Michael and my cousin Johnathan.

My mind was heavy as I dropped Morgan off at the sitter and headed to work. I had a ton of job-related tasks, so my personal matters had to be set aside while I concentrated on them.

During lunch, I made my first call.

"Attorney Vile, this is Jessica," I began. "I'm calling to inquire about my evidentiary letter. Michael said he got his, but I didn't get one."

"You won't get an Evidentiary hearing because there isn't any evidence against you," she said matter-of-factly.

I was in a rage!

"Then why in the hell am I being charged with a crime?"

She didn't respond so I continued.

"Attorney Vile I want my name out of this mess."

"If you would just cooperate and agree to speak with the DEA agents, your name would be out of this mess. As I told you before, I'll be with you the whole time."

"I don't trust them or you," I said. "Therefore, I plead the 5th."

We ended the call.

My next call was to Michael.

"Hey baby," I said.

"What's wrong Jessica?" Michael could hear the frustration in my voice.

I told him what Attorney Vile had said about there not being any evidence against me, and he was just as livid as I had been.

"You need to call the state bar and report her," Michael insisted. "It seems like she is working for the prosecutor and the DEA instead of you!"

I agreed with everything Michael said, but I simply replied, "It probably wouldn't do any good to report her because the entire System seems to be corrupt."

Then I changed the subject momentarily and told Michael about my cousin Johnathan calling and asking me if he could he stay with me temporarily.

After a brief silence, Michael finally said, "It actually would make me feel better for a man to be in the house, but I'll let that decision be yours. I'm fine with whatever is decided."

I hadn't thought about it that way. Morgan and I would probably benefit from having a man in the home.

"Ok," I said. "I'll tell him he can stay and I will only charge him $100 for rent since he's down on his luck right now."

Michael agreed, and then I decided to bring marriage up again.

"I've given your idea about marriage some thought and because of the threats from Attorney Vile and the DEA it probably is best we get married," I said. "Because I refuse to let them and their scare tactics tear our family apart."

Of course, Michael was filled with joy and said, "Let's do it (get married) the next time you and Morgan come to visit me."

"Ok," I said. Now that I'd made the decision, I was beginning to feel good about it.

"That will be the weekend of Grandpa's 100th birthday party celebration. Therefore the timing would be perfect because a lot of my family will be in town."

We talked some more about the wedding and then ended the call. I still needed to contact Johnathan.

Johnathan agreed to the offer and asked if he could move once I got home from work that same day. I told him he could, and we ended the call.

I went back to work filled with all types of emotions, but I didn't have my usual restroom stall breakdown. I contained myself and finished out my workday.

When Morgan and I arrived home, Johnathan was parked in the driveway waiting to move his things in. He only had personal items (clothes, shoes. etc.). He'd put his furniture in storage. Therefore, it didn't take him long to bring his items inside and get settled into his room on the second floor (basement).

Although I was exhausted from my workday, I prepared a meal for myself, Morgan and Johnathan. I figured sitting down to a nice homecooked meal would make Johnathan feel welcomed and give us a chance to talk.

Without going into too much detail, I brought him up to speed regarding the pending legal matter Michael and I were currently facing.

Of course, Johnathan was confused and in a state of shock at the same time.

"Wow cuz," Johnathan said. "I had no idea you had all this going on. Are you ok?"

"I am," I said. "I have to be strong for Morgan's sake."

"Well, I'm not here to make things harder for you. My roommate and I lost our jobs around the same time, and we couldn't make the rent. But I am due to start a new job this coming Monday, so I'll be back on my feet and out of your hair in no time," he promised.

"Thank you, Johnathan," I said. "This will be a blessing for the both of us. You can start paying rent with your first check. I'll get a key made for you tomorrow."

"That will work," Johnathan seemed relieved. "Thanks again for being so generous."

"You're welcome," I said. "By the way, me and Morgan are going back to South Georgia to visit Michael in a week."

I didn't mention the wedding yet.

We finished dinner and Johnathan, and I said our good nights. After cleaning the kitchen, I went to prepare Morgan and myself for bed.

I was thankful the weekend was only a day away!

As I laid restlessly in bed, my mind was filled with thoughts about the unfairness the law was causing upon me and my family.

I also thought about my decision to marry Michael.

I said a prayer and dozed off to sleep.

For Love's Sake

THE NEXT DAY, I got up and went through my normal routine of dropping Morgan off at the sitter and heading to work.

On the way, my phone rings, and it's Michael.

"Hey baby," he begins. "My evidentiary hearing is scheduled for Monday."

"Good," I replied. "I wonder what BS they have conjured up."

"I'm afraid to ask that question," Michael admitted.

"I'm going to call Attorney Vile again on my lunch break," I said. "I know she said I wouldn't be having an Evidentiary Hearing due to the fact there isn't any evidence against me, but I want to see if the story has changed by now."

I ended the call with Michael and walked into work to start my workday. I had several deadlines to meet and time really flew by. I was not looking forward to making the dreadful call to Attorney Vile.

Noon finally arrived, and I phoned Attorney Vile.

"Attorney Vile, why haven't I received a letter regarding my evidentiary hearing," I asked. "Michael has gotten his letter, and his date is set for Monday."

"Like I told you before," she said in what had become her normal mean and condescending tone, "there is no evidence against you."

"Well," I replied angrily, "Why are you having such a difficult time clearing my name and why am I still set to go to trial and why am I still being accused of a crime?"

Attorney Vile clears her throat and says, "All you have to do is agree to talk with the DEA Agents, and your name will be cleared."

"Well," I said simply. "I guess I will be going to trial then. Goodbye."

I was so upset after speaking with Attorney Vile that I had to make a stop by the restroom to not only cry but to also pray and try to gather myself.

I stood in the restroom stall for a good 15 minutes before I returned to my desk. And as usual, I tabled my hurt, stress, and heartache and focused on work as if nothing was wrong and met all of my deadlines with ease.

Finally, the workday came to an end, and I called Michael on my drive to pick up Morgan. I told him about my conversation with Attorney Vile and how upset she had made me.

Of course, then he became upset too and made all kinds of derogatory comments about her and the DEA agents. All of which I agreed with.

"Jessica, I know things look bad now, but they are going to work out in our favor," Michael reassured me.

Sometimes it was hard to see that ending.

"It just seems like they are doing everything in their power to tear our family apart," I said between tears. "I'm just ready to get there and get married."

I had arrived at the sitter's house, so I ended the call with Michael, so I could go inside to get Morgan.

I never thought I would be getting married under these circumstances, I thought to myself. *But I have to keep my family together.*

The weekend arrived, and my plans were to focus on trying to relax, reflect on my life and its present state and prepare mentally for my upcoming nuptials.

Michael and I talked on the phone more than usual. I guess we both were nervous and excited about what was to come in regards to our big day.

The plan for next weekend was for Morgan and me to travel to South Georgia to spend family time with Michael, purchase our wedding rings, get married at the local courthouse, and attend Michael's grandfather 100th birthday celebration.

I had decided to take off the Friday before the wedding/birthday celebration.

Monday morning came quickly, and although the weekend was emotionally taxing, physically I did feel rested. I awoke with a spring in my step.

I prepared Morgan for the sitter and myself for work faster than the I normally did, in fact, I had 30 minutes to spare, which I took advantage of and stopped and got Morgan and myself a little something for breakfast.

Afterwards, I dropped Morgan to the sitter and headed to work.

My music was blasting, and for now, I was in the best mood. I was determined to keep the positive attitude I woke up with.

My phone rang.

"Hey baby," Michael began, "I'm just checking to see that you guys are ok and making it safely to your destinations."

"Yes," I said smiling. "We are ok. Today is a good day."

"I'm happy to hear that," Michael said. "I'm excited about this weekend."

"I am too," I said. "Listen I've made it to work, so I've got to go."

We ended the call, and I went into work to begin my day. There was much to do before taking off that Friday. While the day was busy, it went by fast and soon it was time to go home.

My phone rang before I could pull out of the parking lot. It was Michael.

"How did your day go?"

"It was fine," I replied. Somehow, I knew he was stalling. "What's wrong?"

"Jessica, I know that we are marrying in the midst of an unusual circumstance, but I'm old school and need your father's blessing," Michael said.

"Well," I responded. "Call him."

"Ok," Michael said, and I could tell he was uneasy about it. "I will now."

We ended the call, and I thought, *this entire situation is surreal, but it's my reality, and I must press forward to keep my family together.*

I finally arrived to pick up Morgan. Seeing her smiling face always filled my heart, mind, and soul with nothing but happiness and joy.

Morgan and I made our way home. Once we arrived, I noticed my cousin Johnathan's car parked in the driveway. I was happy since Johnathan and I rarely got to see one another because of his work schedule.

I went inside and got settled a bit and began to prepare dinner while chatting and catching up with Johnathan. I reminded him that I would be in South Georgia this weekend.

I still hadn't told him that I was getting married.

I didn't know how he would feel, and I didn't want to deal with any more negativity than I had too. I knew by now that Michael had spoken with my father and I was wondering how that conversation had gone. I hadn't heard from either of them.

What will I do if my father doesn't give his blessing?

Just what would I do for love?

I realized the choices we make get harder as our circle of love increases.

After dinner, just as I was about to tidy up the kitchen, my phone rang.

It was my father.

A Lesson In The Blessing

HAVE YOU HEARD people say, *I knew it in my spirit?*

I have, and there was a time when it seemed corny to me or even false, but as my phone rang, I knew in my spirit who was calling and why.

LOL

"Jessica," my father began. "I received a call from Michael earlier today. He asked me for your hand in marriage. Are you certain you want to get married?"

My father was not one to beat around the bush, sugar coat, or coddle. He had taught me to do the same. So, I answered him honestly and directly.

"Honestly Dad, I've always pictured myself marrying in an American-dream type wedding, a beautiful fitted white dress, in a church, with all the traditional trimmings," I said sadly. "But the System and the corrupt people that run it are trying to tear my family apart, and I can't allow that to happen. Our goal was to marry one day. I just look at it like this, our current situation has sped up the process. I do love him, and I've witnessed the DEA, and Attorney Vile do nothing but threaten, lie, and try to convince me to turn against Michael. I've told attorney Vile several times to get my name out of this craziness and if Michael has anything to do with it, go after him but leave me out of it. If I marry him, they can't use me against him."

"Well," my father said slowly. "I told Michael I was going to call and talk with you about this. You have my blessing because you are an adult and I support whatever you decide to do."

I ended the call with my father and called Michael and told him of the conversation my father and I just had. Michael and I chatted briefly because it was getting late and we both had to work the next morning.

The rest of the week was uneventful, and soon Friday had arrived.

I woke up at 7:00 am to pack and load our luggage into the car. By 8:30 am, Morgan and I were showered, dressed, and on the road headed to South Georgia.

We stopped to get gas and about an hour into the trip, Michael called.

"Hey baby," Michael said with excitement. "Y'all on the road?"

"Yes, I said," excited too. "We left at 830."

"By the time I get off work, you and Morgan will be at my mom's house waiting for me, and I can't wait to see you both."

"I'm looking forward to it too baby."

"How's the drive going? What time do you think you'll arrive?"

"It's smooth, not much traffic," I responded. "We should get there between 10:30 and 11:00. I'll call and let you know when we make it."

Two and a half hours later, we arrive in the city, and I look in the rearview mirror at Morgan.

"We're here baby girl," I said smiling big. "We're going to see your dad as soon as he gets home from work."

Morgan just smiled back at me.

We were now on the main highway to Michael's mother's house, and I noticed a car leaving the house.

I said to Morgan, "There's your grandma. She must be going to run an errand, so we will go to your Aunt Cindy's house first." Aunt Cindy was a small petite woman. Her house was located down the street from Michael's mother's house.

We pulled up to Aunt Cindy's and found her sitting on the porch. Morgan and I got out, gave hugs, and I said to Aunt Cindy, "I passed by

Jean's (Michael's mom) on the main highway and saw her leaving, so I decided to come here until I think she's made it back home."

Michael's mom, Jean, was a nice lady. She was feisty and spoke her mind. She had a great sense of humor and was strong. When it came to her family, she didn't 'play the radio.' Although we sometimes saw things differently, we got along well.

"That's fine baby," Aunt Cindy said. "Go on inside and get comfortable."

Morgan and I went inside to use the restroom, and to my surprise Aunt Cat, Michael's aunt from Miami was sitting on the couch watching T.V.

"Aunt Cat!" I screamed. "I didn't know you were here! When did you arrive?"

Aunt Cat was my favorite out of all Michael's aunts, and she and I had a very close relationship. She was much like me – she was sweet, kind-hearted and had style. She was strong, and like her sister, Michael's mom, she spoke her mind. She was a gem.

I made a quick run to the restroom, so I could get back to chatting and hugging with my favorite aunt. Aunt Cat and I were chatting away when all of a sudden Aunt Cindy comes in from the porch and says, "I just heard a big boom that sounded like a bad accident. Sound like it came from where Jean lives. Jessica, will you go up there and make sure everything is ok?"

"Ok," I said. Morgan, Aunt Cat and I got in my car and went up the street to check things out. Aunt Cindy had been right. The big boom she heard had been a bad accident involving Michael's mother Jean and a Comcast van.

Jean's car was sitting in her yard with the trunk of the car completely smashed in, and the Comcast van was in the ditch on the opposite side of the road.

My heart dropped to the pit of my stomach as I pulled up, parked and grabbed Morgan. Then we all ran over toward Jean's car.

There were a few people already gathered there, and they stopped us before we made it to the driver's door of the car.

A guy from the crowd said, "She's ok. The ambulance has been called. We aren't going to move her from the car though. We will let the paramedics do that."

Aunt Cat called out to her sister, "Jean, you ok?"

"I'm ok Cat," Jean responded in a soft voice.

Hearing Jean's voice calmed my heart just a little.

Then another person from the crowd says, "The ambulance needs to hurry and get here so they can get those kids from the back seat of the car."

I could feel my eyes stretch as I screamed out, "Oh my God, the babies are in the car."

Michael's niece and nephew were in the car. The entire crowd began to shush me and said, "They're ok. They are just sleeping. Jean took them to get shots at the doctor today.

I immediately *shushed,* but I was still hysterical inside. I began to sweat and breathe hard. I took a few steps back to phone Michael and told him he needed to get off from work and come home immediately.

I tried my best to remain calm while talking to Michael, but it was really hard.

"Jessica, what's wrong," Michael insisted.

"Just get home now Michael," I said. I was trying not to alarm him but wanted him to know it was urgent.

"Jessica just be straight with me," Michael pleaded.

"It's Jean," I began. "She's been in an accident, but she is ok."

"Are you being straight with me Jessica? Is my mother ok?"

"Yes, Michael she is. The paramedics are on the way."

"I am too," Michael said and ended the call.

I had decided not to tell him about the children being trapped in the back seat of the car.

"Has Ben been notified," I asked someone in the crowd. Ben was Michael's brother, the children's father.

No one seemed to know, so I called him and told him.

"Me and Eva just left Jean and the kids," Ben said in a slow country drawl. "She picked them up for us from the doctor because we had to get back to work."

Ben and his wife Eva worked for the same company on the same shift. Eva was short, quiet, young, and complemented Ben's southern gentleman spirit.

"Is it bad?" Ben asked.

I could tell that Ben was hysterical. He was asking questions instead of trying to get here.

"The accident happened right in front of Jean's house," I told him. "Just get here immediately."

I ended the call with Ben and noticed that the paramedics had finally arrived. Jean was rescued from the car first. Then the jaws of life crew hooked their machine up to the trunk area of the car to rescue the kids. The newborn who was in a rear-facing car seat was rescued next. The crew then went to the other side of the car where the four-year-old little girl sat in a front-facing car seat. I noticed the medical helicopter land, and I thought to myself someone must be seriously injured. The tears begin to flow; I couldn't hold back my emotions.

I didn't make a sound, but I cried quietly.

Finally, they rescued the 4-year-old.

The paramedics immediately removed her from her car seat and started CPR on her. She was unresponsive as they loaded her into the medical helicopter.

I phoned Ben again and told him to just go to the hospital because his mom and kids were being taken to the hospital.

He replied, "ok."

Michael still hadn't made it home from work yet. He worked about 45 minutes to an hour away depending on traffic.

Aunt Cat, Morgan and I sat in the car and waited for Michael so that we could go to the hospital together.

News of the accident had started to spread because lots of people were starting to show up at the house inquiring.

Michael finally arrived home. He jumped in the car with us (Aunt Cat, Morgan, myself) and we headed to the hospital. I gave Michael the details of the accident on the drive to the hospital.

Michael was a bit upset with me because I hadn't told him how bad of an accident it was when I called to inform him. I replied, "I didn't want you driving like a bat out of hell trying to get home, and something happened to you."

We pull up to the hospital and see Ben in the parking lot crying hysterically and throwing everything from his vehicle out on the ground.

His wife Eva and a small crowd of people surrounded him. I said to Michael, "Something bad has happened."

We all jumped out the car and asked, "What's wrong?"

That's when Ben screamed, "My baby girl is gone."

My entire insides went numb. All I could say as I cried hysterically was, "I thought everyone was going to be ok."

Although Ben and Michael had different fathers, no two brothers were closer. Ben looked up to

Michael and eventually it was Michael who was able to calm him down enough to return inside the hospital. The doctor informed Ben and his wife that their baby girl died from a hairline fracture in her skull.

Jean and the newborn (Tyler) would have to stay in the hospital for a couple days, but they were going to be fine.

There was a witness to the accident at the hospital who informed us that Jean was turning into her yard. She had her signal on and out of nowhere a speeding Comcast van comes along and rams right into the back of her. The force pushed her car into her yard, and the van landed in the ditch on the opposite side of the road. He stated he had told the officer on scene everything he witnessed.

We were at the hospital until almost midnight before heading home. Once we arrived back to Michael's mother's house, I said to Michael, "Maybe this is a sign we shouldn't get married."

"Maybe it's a sign that we should," Michael quickly replied. "Everyone didn't die. There has got to be a lesson in that blessing."

With the pending court case and all that had happened and now this, I didn't understand how Michael could say that. I was too outdone with today's tragedy to even defend my position, so I simply replied ok and prepared Morgan and myself for bed.

In The Blink of An Eye

MORNING CAME super-fast. It was if I had just laid down. My eyes were swollen from crying so much the day before.

Michael and I had to be to the courthouse by noon, and we still needed to purchase the rings. I got dressed but wasn't feeling beautiful or like a bride.

Yesterday had really taken a toll on me.

Michael realized that I was emotionally drained and got Morgan dressed after he finished dressing himself.

Two of his cousins, Shay and Tim, would be our witnesses for the ceremony. We stopped by Aunt Cindy's house to pick Shay up. Tim would meet us at the courthouse.

Let me be honest here, I looked a *hot damn mess,* but I was determined to go with the flow.

We made one more stop on the way to the courthouse, and that was to a local drug/pharmacy store that sold among other things, jewelry. Here is where we purchased our rings.

"Ya'll getting yall rings from a drug store?" Michael's cousin Shay asked.

I smirked and said, "I guess so."

"Shut up Shay," Michael laughed. "There's a jewelry department inside too."

On April 29, 2007, Michael and I arrived at the courthouse, went inside, stood before the Justice of the Peace and with Morgan and our witnesses by our side, we got married.

At the end of the ceremony, the Justice of the Peace asked, "Well, do you feel married?"

"Not yet," I stated. "I won't know until I create my first honey-do list."

We all chuckled.

By the time our wedding ceremony was over, it was time for Michael's grandpa Henry's 100th birthday celebration to begin.

I really thought the birthday celebration and my wedding would have been canceled after the horrific accident that took place the day before. But it seems I was the only one who felt that way. Maybe they wanted something triumphant to focus on besides the tragedy.

We arrived at the celebration, and the mood, of course, was extremely somber. Everyone seemed to still be in a state of shock.

A few hours into the celebration, Ben and his wife show up. They looked really out of it. My heart just melted with sadness just looking at them, because I could see the hurt and pain in their eyes.

After the celebration, we said our goodbyes and went back to Michael's mom's house.

I prepared Morgan for bed early so that Michael and I could have some alone time to talk about the things that had transpired and the upcoming legal woes.

Morgan and I would be returning home to Atlanta the next morning.

"Do you think your attorney can file a motion with the court to allow you to return home now that we're married," I asked hopefully.

"I don't know, but I plan to phone her on Monday to ask."

"Michael, I don't feel like a blushing bride," I confessed. "The circumstances under which we got married, and the car accident just places a cloud of sadness over a day that should be happy."

"I'm sad too Jessica," Michael said. "But things are going to get better and will work out in our favor. We can't give up on living."

I nodded my head in agreement, but my heart still felt an overwhelming sense of sadness.

"I just know that the judge will see through all of the lies and lack of evidence the prosecutor and the DEA agents have used to trump up these charges against us," Michael said confidently. "And as for us getting married, well it happened sooner than we planned, but I'm happy about it."

Again, I nodded in agreement.

Although Michael felt good about getting married, I didn't, but I kept saying to myself, "I can't let my family get torn apart."

I found solace in that thought and kept pushing forward in spite of all the hell that was breaking loose around me.

It was after 11 pm. Michael and I chatted a few more minutes, and finally, he drifted off to sleep.

I lay there thinking about how our lives can change in the blink of an eye.

A Waste of Time

SUNDAY MORNING ARRIVES and its time for me and Morgan to return home.

Michael packed the car while I prepared Morgan and myself for the trip back home.

It was always sad to say goodbye, but this time was harder because now I was a married woman leaving my husband. My daughter's father wasn't coming with us.

We stood and hugged and kissed for more than ten minutes. No one wanted to let go.

The weekend had been bittersweet.

An hour into the drive, the weekend's events began to replay over and over in my mind. This went on for the entire ride home.

I really pray that Michael calls me tomorrow with the good news of him going to court and that they are allowing him to return home now that we are married, I thought.

Morgan and I arrived home safely.

I quickly called Michael to let him know we were safely home and then ended the call to unpack and prepare for the upcoming week.

I was exhausted both emotionally and physically.

It felt like I hadn't slept in weeks. I crawled into bed and sleep came over me swiftly.

Although I had fallen asleep quickly, I woke up all throughout the night. I found myself tossing and turning with what felt like the weight of the world on my shoulders.

The next morning, it was time to rise and grind.

On my way to drop Morgan to the sitter, my phone rings. It's Michael, checking on Morgan and me.

We spoke briefly, and I ended the call and took Morgan inside to the sitter and headed to work.

Before heading to the office, I stopped by HR to complete a name change form. I was now Jessica Alvin.

Once I got to work, I felt tired from the restless night, but as usual, I pushed past those feelings and put my best foot forward and handled my work day.

How do I let my co-workers know that I got married over the weekend, I wondered?

I knew they would have all sorts of questions. The good thing was, I was known for being private, so I was confident I would be able to shut all evasive questions down nicely with a smile.

I logged into my work computer and immediately changed my last name on my work email signature block. That was one way to get the word out.

As I began to reply to emails, as I expected, the questions regarding my new last name started to roll in.

"I got married over the weekend," I responded simply.

The questioning went on all day as I knew it would. And my answer remained the same, "Yes, I got married over the weekend."

There were a few co-workers that I shared a bit more with. But only the fact that it was a planned courthouse wedding.

Noon quickly arrived, and it was lunchtime. My phone rang, and it was Attorney Vile.

"I hear that you're married now," Attorney Vile said.

"Yea," I said matching her cool tone. "I'm now Mrs. Michael Alvin."

"The DEA agents are livid," she told me. "Be prepared to go to trial."

"Ok," I replied ok and hung up.

I immediately phoned Michael to tell him about Attorney Vile's call.

Michael was angry.

"I spoke with my attorney too," he said. "She told me that it was a waste of time because you and I weren't married before being indicted. Therefore, the court will never approve of me returning home."

I could feel the anger and tears building up inside of me.

I pulled myself together and told Michael everything was going to be ok because the court will see through the lies the DEA agents have constructed. Michael agreed and began telling me that his mother and his nephew were released from the hospital. I was happy to hear that.

I ended the call with Michael and made a stop by the restroom to cry out to God for strength.

Once I was inside the restroom stall, I had a major breakdown, silently of course. I stood in one place as tears rolled from my eyes profusely and nonstop. I looked up so that my Heavenly Father could fill me with His strength to remain strong in spite of what was going on around me.

After about 10 minutes or so I was calm and composed and returned to my office to finish out the workday. I was able to complete my work tasks and attend meetings before my day finally ended.

All I could think about as I walked to my car was those mini breakdown bathroom stall sessions with God were miracles letting me know that He hears my cry and He's with me.

On my drive to get Morgan I replayed the day's events over in my head, but I refused to let them consume me and put me back in a funk.

"I've got to stay upbeat for Morgan," I said trying to encourage myself. "She may be just a toddler, but I know she senses my mood."

I arrive at the babysitter's to pick up the love of my life. I hug and kiss her fat cheeks and use that time with my daughter to mask all the negative thoughts and conversations that had taken place earlier in my day.

When Morgan and I arrived home, I busied myself with what had become a normal routine (cooking, eating, preparing for bed, etc.).

Later when it was finally time to rest my mind, body, and soul, I prayed to God for a peaceful night's sleep because the day had been a day of disappointments.

Jacked-Up Circumstances

THE NEXT FIVE MONTHS of my life were a whirlwind of activity centered around me being a long-distance wife to Michael, traveling to South Georgia with Morgan and getting threatening messages from my so-called attorney and the DEA agents.

The Prosecutor and the DEA were really upset with me for marrying Michael. Their plan had been to use threats and fear tactics to get me to testify against Michael in court.

Whenever Attorney Vile contacted me with a *nastygram* from the DEA, my reply was always, "If Michael did what he's being accused of then get him for what he did and leave me out of it."

Now that Michael and I were married they had to come up with another scheme of lies to present in court.

September 2007, I finally received a letter in the mail regarding our court date. Court was scheduled for October 1, 2007, which was a Wednesday. Although it had been almost a year since the start of this entire ordeal, reality hit me like a ton of bricks.

I've been convicted of a crime I didn't commit, I thought, *and I'm going to trial although there is no evidence against me.*

I thought to myself, *only in America can a person be labeled guilty and have to prove their innocence.*

My mind immediately switched to concern over my employment. *What in the world was I going to say to my employer in regards to needing time off for trial?* For this entire year, I had been successful at keeping my secret. No one at my job knew anything about what had been going on in my personal life. I decided to phone Attorney Vile.

"I finally got a court date," I said hoping that by now she would be willing to be an asset for me.

"I've been notified," she said simply. "Meet me at the courthouse on the date and time reflected in the letter."

"OK," I said hesitantly. "But shouldn't you and I meet prior to trial to prepare and go over the particulars because this will be my first time being on trial."

"No," Attorney Vile said simply, "that's not necessary."

I ended the call and thought to myself, *what a waste of my father's money.* I might as well have chosen to be represented by a *Public Pretender* (that's what I call public defenders)!

I called Michael to tell him about my conversation with Attorney Vile and her nonchalant attitude.

"I'm not surprised," Michael said clearly upset. "They've made it up in their mind that we are guilty and so they aren't even trying to fight for us. But don't you worry Jessica, things will be ok once we get to court. The judge will see how we've been railroaded."

I prayed he was right. We ended the call, and I spent time meditating on how to ask for time off for the trial.

Monday morning seemed to arrive faster than usual. I awoke in a positive mood and decided to play some gospel music as I prepared Morgan for the sitter and myself for work. I figured some good gospel would keep my positive aura flowing.

I dropped Morgan to the sitter and drove to work listening and singing my gospel, then all of a sudden, my phone rings. It's Michael doing his normal morning check-in on Morgan and me.

I assured him we were fine. We chatted a while longer and ended the call.

Once at work, I immediately completed the paperwork requesting the day off I needed to attend court. I had to list a reason for my request, so I wrote that I needed to attend to a personal matter concerning my mom. I only requested one day because I figured once the trial was over, I would return to work the next day even though I had to drive 2 ½ to 3 hours because the court was in South Georgia. My supervisor immediately approved my time off request and expressed empathy for me having to be there for my mom. I felt so guilty for lying about why I was requesting time off but was too embarrassed to let my supervisor in on the real deal.

For the rest of the week, I worked really hard and made sure all my tasks were completed for the current week and the following week because I would be out of office that Wednesday and didn't want to fall behind.

On the drive home from work, I phoned my aunt Vera (my mother's oldest sister and my cousin Johnathan's mom) who lived in South Georgia and asked her to watch Morgan while I attended court next Wednesday. Aunt Vera happily agreed.

My plan was to have Morgan and my bags packed and drive to South Georgia Tuesday after work.

I finally arrived to pick up Morgan from the sitter. We made our way home to carry out our normal routine. Later that night I spoke with Michael and informed him of my plan, to which he agreed. The rest of my work week was pretty normal besides a little nervousness in my stomach which was to be expected due to all of the chaos I had going on personally.

The weekend came and went in what seemed like the blink of an eye.

Tuesday morning, I loaded our luggage in the car, dropped Morgan off to the sitter and then headed to work. I was nervous but more anxious over finally putting this trial behind us and getting on with our lives. I completed my workday like I'd planned, ahead of the game so-to-speak, and finally, picked up Morgan, and we traveled to South Georgia.

I was excited I would get to see Michael although it would be under *jacked up* circumstances.

Two and a half hours later, Morgan and I arrived safely to Michael's mother's house. We both had huge smiles on our faces as Michael walked up to the car. We went inside and just sat, talked and enjoyed each other's company for a couple of hours before we finally prepared for bed. We had to be at the courthouse early the next morning. According to the letter, trial proceedings would begin promptly at 9:00 am.

6:00 am Wednesday morning, I woke up with an extremely nervous stomach. I got dressed for court and prepared Morgan to go to my Aunt Vera's while Michael, his mother and I attended court. We left home at 7:30 am, dropped Morgan off at Aunt Vera's and made our way to the courthouse which was about a 20-minute drive.

We pulled up to the courthouse, and my first thoughts were, *welcome to Mayberry*. The courthouse was a small, country, hick-looking place. We walk inside the courthouse, and I see my attorney for the first time since I hired her.

Attorney Vile is a tall, heavy-set, plain-Jane, butch-looking woman. She looks at me, and I look at her. My initial vibe of her isn't a good one. She seems sneaky and evil — not a good first impression. Finally, I decide to be the bigger person and walk over to her.

"Good morning," I said cordially, "So what do I do? Where do I sit?"

She mustered up enough strength (seems like it was hurting her to talk to me) and replied with simple instructions. I conducted myself accordingly.

There was a total of five defendants in attendance: myself, Michael, Michael's mom, a friend of Michael's and a woman I didn't know. We all sat together on one bench even though we had our own separate attorneys. All the attorneys sat together on another bench. The Judge called the court to order, and the proceedings began. When the Judge called our name, we had to stand as well as the attorney representing us to show we were in attendance.

The next thing to take place was selecting a jury. The attorneys and the Prosecutor were the only ones that got to participate in the jury selection. Us defendants weren't allowed to say a word. The jury selection process consisted of the jurors being asked questions such as, "Have you ever had any run-ins with the police?", "Have you been predisposed to the case via newspaper, word of mouth, etc.?" and "Do you feel you can be fair and unbiased if selected to be a juror on a drug case?"

Every juror that had a run-in with the law or knew someone that had wasn't selected. This process was finally completed at noon. The judge instructed everyone to take an hour for lunch, and the court would reconvene at 1:00 pm.

Michael, his mother and I walked to a fast food restaurant just a couple of feet down from the courthouse. This all seemed surreal to me. It was like a bad dream that I wished someone would pinch and awake me from. During lunch, we talked about how biased that juror selection process was. I really didn't eat much; I guess it was due to my nerves.

As we made our way back to the courthouse, we crossed paths with the Prosecutor, DEA agents, and our attorneys coming back from lunch together. The look and the evil smirks on the faces of some of them was very unsettling to me.

We returned to the courtroom, and the trial began.

Every witness the Prosecutor called was someone from the case who had been offered and had taken a plea deal. All the attorneys were cross-examining the witnesses except for mine because I didn't know any of the witnesses and they didn't know me. It was obvious that each witness was coached with what to say because although the Prosecutor asked questions first, when the attorneys crossed-examined, asking more details in regards to the same questions just posed by the Prosecutor, the witnesses would just give a blank stare and stutter, "ah...ah...I don't know," and laugh. It was like being in a circus full of clowns.

Of course, I wasn't allowed to talk or say a mumbling word throughout this farce of a so-called trial. I would make eye contact with Michael and his mother, and we all had the same look of shock, confusion, and disbelief on our faces.

You could hear giggles and mummers throughout the courtroom which made me take a look around, and to my surprise, it was coming from the courtroom staff. This was a testament to how ridiculously coached the witnesses sounded; even the courtroom staff found it absurdly funny.

I also noticed that the court reporter's facial expressions were of disbelief as she transcribed. I sat there thinking, *there is no justice in this so-called justice system. My life and freedom (and the lives and freedom of others) were on the line, and yet this proceeding is being handled like a joke. This has to only happen in a Mayberry, hick-town court.*

As time ticked away, the testimonies of the witnesses got more and more outrageous. Finally, the Prosecutor stated he didn't have any more witnesses to call and the Attorneys state they didn't have any witness or anything else to say so the judge said his final words and instructed all in attendance that court proceedings would reconvene tomorrow at 9:00 am.

I thought to myself, *what!!!!!!! I have to be back at work tomorrow. I only requested one day off.*

Court was now adjourned, so I walked up to Attorney Vile and told her of the dilemma with my job.

You need to take off the rest of the week," she replied coolly, "because the trial will probably last until Friday."

I looked up at her with a deep, intense gaze and thought to myself, *this is some bullshit. She could have communicated this to me earlier.*

I shook off the gaze, didn't say a word, and just walked away from her. I went to find Michael and his mom, so we could leave. We stopped to pick up Morgan from Aunt Vera on the way home. I was so glad to see my angel's smiling face.

Michael, his mom and I shared our thoughts about the trial with one another on the ride home. We were in agreement about how the day's court proceedings were circus-like and that there was no way the jury didn't see through the *BS*. We were certain that would work in our favor.

I phoned my Supervisor as soon we reached home but got her voicemail instead.

"Jess, this is Jessica," I said trying to keep the tremble out of my voice. "I will be out until Friday. The situation with my mom is taking longer than I expected. I will return to work on Monday."

I hung up and thought to myself, *I'll be glad when this is over, and my life returns to normal.*

The Book of Job

DAY TWO OF THE TRIAL is only more of the same clown-type witnesses as the day before. The only difference is that the prosecutor plays an unclear recording. The only thing that could be heard and understood was a male's voice saying something about jeans to which the Prosecutor explains, "Jeans are drugs, and the guy in the recording is Michael."

They had a witness to corroborate this story. She also stated that I was with Michael at this particular *jean* transaction. I was immediately filled with anger and nearly fell out of my seat. The Prosecutor then asked her to point Michael and me out, and she did.

Attorney Vile (my attorney) crossed examined the woman, but it wasn't in my favor at all.

"Are you sure that Jessica was with Michael on the day of the *jean* transaction?"

"Yes," the witness said and nodded her head. "She and I talked during the transaction."

"Can you point her out to us," Attorney Vile asked.

She did.

"I have no further questions," Attorney Vile said and returned to the attorney's table.

The judge called for a recess. I immediately walked over to Attorney Vile.

"Put me on the stand," I insisted. "Let me speak up for myself since you didn't."

"No," she replied, "you will not be testifying. The Prosecutor will eat you alive."

I walked off burning up on the inside thinking, *this bitch help set me up.* I recalled the threat she made to me saying, "If you don't talk to the DEA agents, they will put someone on the stand to say you were involved," and that is exactly what happened.

Recess was over, and as I headed back to the courtroom, I walked passed the Prosecutor. He had a stupid smirk on his face as if to say, *I told you so,* without actually saying it. I gave him the *if looks could kill look* and kept it moving.

The court was now back in session, and a few more coached witnesses were called to which all the attorneys except for mine cross-examined. Michael's attorney was the only attorney that seemed to be asking questions that called the witnesses out on their lies. All the other attorneys pretty much asked questions to support the witnesses' lies.

The Judge called for any more witnesses etc. and there weren't any, so the court was adjourned until the next day (Friday) at 9:00 am.

I was so upset leaving the courthouse, and I expressed it the entire drive to pick-up Morgan.

"That's why it took them a year to bring this case to court," I said almost yelling. "They schemed and pieced together this bullshit story that would work in their favor. There are no pictures, no concrete evidence, just lying coached witnesses who were promised time off of their sentences if they cooperated with the authorities."

Day three of court was for the attorneys to present their closing arguments to the jury. During the closing arguments, my attorney's argument was short and quick.

"One witness' testimony," she said flatly, "stating my client was present at a *jean* transaction isn't enough to find her guilty."

The Prosecutor followed with his arguments against me and totally killed my character and creditability to the jury.

"All Jessica likes to do," he said smugly, "is dress in fancy clothes and ride in her live-in boyfriend's black SUV. She's an unfit and irresponsible parent as evident by allowing her child to be present during a drug transaction as one witness attested."

To have to sit there and listen to the things said about me and not able to utter a word in my defense was torture. It felt like my soul was being ripped out of my body. They never told the jurors I worked at a full-time professional job, or that I was three weeks away from graduating with my B.S. degree, or that I had an interview scheduled for Monday morning for a higher salaried position.

I could feel the tears forming in my eyes. I tried with all my might to hold them back but couldn't. I made eye contact with Michael, and he was gazing at me with sadness in his face and tears in his eyes too.

The Prosecutor ripped the other defendants to shreds as he had done me and then the Judge dismissed the jurors to go decide whether we five defendants were guilty or not guilty. Court was in recess until the jury was ready with their decision.

Forty-five minutes later the jury came back with guilty verdicts for all five of us.

The judge released us to the custody of the US Marshalls. I was crying hysterically. All I could do was think about my Morgan. We were escorted to the back of the courthouse and placed in waiting rooms.

"Jessica," Michael was yelling out to me. "It's going to be alright. Be strong."

I was crying so hard and so much, I heard him, but I didn't hear him.

Michael and his friend were shackled and taken away by the Marshalls. Me, Michael's mom and Kristen (the woman I didn't know) sat in a room awaiting our Marshall pickup.

I later learned that unlike the other 33 people associated with our case, Kristen had opted to go to trial instead of taking a plea deal. Kristen was tall, pretty, dark-skinned, and had long hair. I also came to learn that although she was married to someone else, she was the girlfriend of the head guy on this case who hadn't been caught by the authorities yet.

The things we do for love.

The next set of Marshalls came and shackled Kirsten and I and hauled us off the county jail. I was still crying hysterically, and Kristen was smiling and laughing and waving goodbye to her family as we were being loaded into the back of the Marshall car. I thought to myself; *she must be on drugs because nothing about this situation is funny.*

We arrived at the county jail and was placed in a holding cell filled with other females while we waited for the transportation van to take us to the jail where we would be housed until it was time for us to come back to court for sentencing.

The females that were in the cell kept complementing Kristen and me on how nice we were dressed and asked if we just came from court. They kept saying, "Yall are a couple of bad bitches." In their eyes, *bad bitches* was a term of endearment. I didn't respond and turned deaf to anything that came out of their mouths.

About an hour later we were loaded into the transportation van with some male inmates who were going to the same jail where we would be housed. Kristen talked, laughed and joked with the male inmates for the entire ride. I think she knew a few of them because they were all from South Georgia. I was the only one on the van who lived in Atlanta. I didn't talk to any of them. They were asking my name, and I replied with the look of death, and they eventually got the picture. I did hear one of them asked Kristen if I was on the case with her and said that he'd never seen me before.

We finally arrived at the jail where we would be housed, it was near Augusta, GA. The female jailer that checked me in kept asking me what I was in for and each time she asked, I wanted to respond, "Nothing," because I didn't do anything to be there, but I knew if I replied with that, she wouldn't believe me.

She said, "You look so nice. You don't have to tell me what you did; I'll look it up."

I burst into tears, and she took me to a room where I had to undress, squat and cough at the same time which was tremendously humiliating. I felt angry, hurt, mortified and in disbelief over that fact that my rights had been violated.

The jailer then informed me that I did get one phone call. I called my mom.

"Jessica," my mom cried with relief. "Where are you? What's going on? Vera said you all were found guilty and taken to jail!"

All I could do was cry. I felt so weak, alone and powerless. My mother cried with me and tried to be encouraging as much as she could.

"Don't you worry baby. This will all get cleared up. In the meantime, you be strong. And don't worry about Morgan. I'll go get her and keep her with me until things get resolved."

I knew Morgan was in good hands with my sweet Aunt Vera. Aunt Vera was not only kind and a true southern bell, but she was loyal to family. However, knowing that my mother would be caring for her while I dealt with this situation gave me a real sense of peace.

"Thank you, mom," I said through my tears. "I love you and Dad." I ended the call.

Another jailer arrived and escorted Kristen and me to our cell. When we entered the cell, there were women in the sitting area playing cards. Two of them stood up and began arguing and yelling at one another. I thought to myself, *what in the hell have I gotten myself into.*

The jailer walked us upstairs and showed us the cell we would share. There were two cemented bunk beds with green mats serving as the mattress, a toilet and a shower that was separate. The jailer gave us the house rules so-to-speak and then left us to get acquainted with our new living quarters and the other ladies.

I went downstairs to the sitting room where the other ladies were gathered, but I didn't say much, I just sat quietly with my thoughts and pretended to watch TV. Night came really quick, and it was time for us to go to our cells. A few minutes later the cell doors slammed shut.

The sound of the cell door slamming sent eerie chills through me. I cried all night long and didn't sleep well at all.

I spent the next day making phone calls. I called my mom and told her to contact my job and tell them I would not be back and if they asked why do not tell them. Next, I called my father to see if he could hire me a new attorney. My father replied that he would see what he could do.

I was so anxious and wanted out of that jail immediately.

"What happens if you can't hire me a new attorney?"

"Well, I guess you will just have to go to prison."

"The devil is a lie," I said and ended the call.

I immediately asked a few ladies where I could get some paper and a pen. One of them gave me some paper and a pen and added that I owed her nothing because she understood how it was when you first arrive to jail, "It takes a couple days to receive money, so you can buy paper, pens, canteen, etc."

I thank her and rushed to my cell and wrote letters to the NAACP and the Rainbow Coalition. I planned to mail the letters as soon as my family put money on my books.

After writing my letters, I took a closer look at what I decided to consider my new 'temporary' surroundings and the ladies that I was incarcerated with.

My cellmate Kristen and I developed a closeness. When one of us was feeling down, the other would be encouraging. Kristen shared with me that her parents were very spiritual. One day after she had spoken with them via phone, she told me they ask her to tell me to read the book of JOB. I was raised in the church but had never actually read an entire book of the Bible.

The next day I called my mom to check on her and my daughter. She informed me all was well and told me that one of my co-worker's called her back.

"She wanted to know what was going on because she said you were not the type to just resign like that," Mom said. "Jessica, she sounded like she really cared. I told her I had to check with you first before I divulged your personal business."

"Call her back," I said with confidence. "Tell her what has happened. Maybe they can help me."

"I will baby," Mom said, happy at the thought of allies. "Me, your father, your sister, and your nephew drove up to Atlanta to pack up your house. We put all of your things in storage."

Mom told me that my cousin Johnathan had moved out and that we had now lost the house. I was saddened but decided to look at it positively having read the story of Job the night before. *When I'm free, I'll get it all back and then some,* I reasoned.

My mom put Morgan on the phone, and I called her Scooterpeas (one of my nicknames for her), and to my surprise, she giggled. She recognized my voice. I was overjoyed.

"I love you," I said.

"I love you," Morgan replied back.

I was in awe. I didn't expect to hear that because she was only speaking single words before our separation. God knew I needed to hear that. Michael and I always told Morgan we loved her, so she was used to hearing it. Mom returned to the phone after she heard my excitement and before I could tell her what Morgan said, she said, "I heard her say she loves you." Mom was tickled pink as well.

Before ending the call, mom told me she had put money in my account. I thanked her, and we said our goodbyes. I decided to spend the rest of my day reading the Bible.

I continued with the book of JOB.

Relationship and Religion

I **DIDN'T PARTAKE** in lots of things the ladies in my cell block were into. Reading the Bible was a better fit for me because the games the ladies played were, in my opinion, childish. For instance, the ladies would play this game called OUT where they made a mini ball out of several socks rolled together, and one person would throw it at the others and whoever got hit was "IT." I refused to play. The ladies would ask me to join, and every time I would reply, "When I was a child, I did childish things, now that I'm an adult I've put away my childish ways."

Of course, they gave me grief about not being fun, but it didn't bother me one bit because I refuse to lay down my class and dignity just because I was in jail. I finished the book of JOB and now understood why Kristen's parents told me to read it.

JOB's story reminded me of my current situation. Different circumstances but a story filled with trials and test. From that day forward, I read the Bible every day.

A month goes by, and I've seen, heard and witnessed the most hurt, anger, dysfunction I'd ever experienced in my life. Things that I thought only existed in movies, I came to realize were real.

The ladies knew this was my first time in jail but for some reason, every night before bedtime one or a few of them would come to me and ask would I say a prayer for them for various reasons like if they were going to court the next day, or had family issues, etc. etc. My reply would be, "I pray for all of us every night."

And then they would respond, "I know but would you say a special one for me."

"Ok," I'd simply reply. They thought I was so strong, but they had no idea that every night when I took my shower, I would break down and cry out to God asking Him why He had allowed this bad thing to happen to me.

What did I do? Had I been a bad person?

I couldn't understand why I was there, and I certainly couldn't understand what they saw in me. I was in jail right next to them!

I was going through what they were going through, but like always, I grieved in private; crying out to God questioning His plan for my life. I don't know what they saw in me, but I was going through it.

However, as always, I held my pain in until I felt it was appropriate to let it out.

One Sunday I decided to attend church. I walked into the room where church service was being held, and the Minister walked up to me and shook my hand and introduced herself as Minister Williams. I came to know her as a true woman of God. She was classy, elegant, a survivor and later I learned an overcomer of her own trials and tribulations. I imagine it is the challenges in life that help to make us strong.

As I was stating my name, she continued to hold my hand and said, "You are truly anointed."

I just smiled and said, "Thank you." I didn't understand what she meant, but I did know it wasn't anything bad. I never thought I would enjoy a jailhouse church service, but to my surprise I did. I enjoyed it more than I had attending church on the outside.

My world had been rocked, so God had my full attention.

Towards the end of the service, Minister Williams asked if anyone wanted to give their life to Christ today and I stood up and went to the front, and she prayed for me. I accepted Christ as my personal Lord and Savior. From that day forward, I began to learn the difference between *relationship* and *religion*.

I called my mom once I got back to the cell block to tell her about church service and what happened to me during the service. She was glad to see me in good spirits and went on to inform me that she had received 17 character reference letters from my co-workers on my behalf. I was so overjoyed I started to cry. I told mom the letters would help me during sentencing. I asked her to thank everyone for me.

The fact that I was willing to allow my coworkers to know what was happening to me was an indication that I'd grown stronger spiritually.

I experienced my first toothache. It was so bad I had to submit a medical request and be taken to an outside dentist, shackled and escorted by a local deputy. I was humiliated because when we arrived at the dentist office, I was taken through the back door, so I wouldn't scare the patients. The dentist eventually checked my tooth and filled it; all the while I was in handcuffs and shackles.

On the way back to the jail the deputy offered me a stick of gum.

"What are you in here for?" He asked.

"Nothing heinous," I said with a stiff smile.

He let it go and didn't pry but shocked me with his next words.

"You look like a nice lady," he said, "when you get out of here can I contact you?"

You have no idea how disgusted with people who wear badges and are affiliated with the law I am, I thought. But of course, I couldn't say that. So, I replied, "I don't know when I'm going to get out."

"Ok," he said. "I'll keep checking."

Thank God the jail wasn't far from the dentist office because I was ready to get away from him. I returned to my cellblock and rested the rest of the day.

That night before bedtime I decided to call my mom. I needed to hear Morgan's voice. As I was talking with Morgan the ladies seemed to be getting louder (talking, laughing) so I politely turned and asked them if they could keep it down because I couldn't hear. The loud laughing and talking didn't cease so again I politely turned and asked the ladies would they please keep it down. I waited a few minutes, and it still continued. Finally, I snapped.

I turned around and yelled to the top of my lungs, "Will ya'll shut the fuck up!"

Everyone stopped what they were doing and just stared at me. One of the ladies said, "Oh my I didn't know you had that in you."

"I said it politely twice," I said. "Seems like no one was listening until I got rude."

I had their full attention, and they gave me the quiet I asked for. I enjoyed the rest of my call, and no one said a word. I got a few dirty looks, but I didn't care.

Three months into my incarceration and I was maintaining well for the most part. I spent my days reading the Bible, writing letters to Michael and attending church on Sundays. A week into my 3rd month, I finally received a letter about my sentencing hearing which was scheduled to take place on January 25, 2008. That would make 3 months and 21 days in the county jail for me.

I phoned my mom to tell her about my sentencing court date. She and my father didn't attend my trial because they had no idea I would be railroaded like I was, but hell and high water couldn't keep them from my sentencing.

"Send me some clothes to wear home," I said confidently to my mom. I've always been a believer in speaking things into existence.

"Ok," Mom said. She was used to me and knew just to accept it and move on. We ended the call.

My father hadn't been able to hire me a new attorney, so Attorney Vile remained in place as my so-called representative.

January 25, 2018, I prepare for sentencing. I had the clothing my mom sent to me, so I didn't have to wear the prison issues orange inmate jumper. But I did have to be shackled along with the others.

I looked great, but my hair was a mess!

The four-hour van ride from the jail to the courthouse seemed to take forever, but finally, we arrived. I was shackled to Kristen, and we were escorted inside the courtroom. As I sat down on the bench I looked over and saw Michael, his mom and friend already seated.

The judge called us up one by one with our attorneys. I was the last person to be sentenced. It was now Attorney Vile's and my turn to approach the bench. And to my surprise instead of the Judge handing down my sentence, he said, "You were there the day of the "Jean" transaction as the witness testified during the trial and you need to admit it."

I looked at the judge and shook my head, "no."

He looked at Attorney Vile and said, "You need to make your client aware of the seriousness that she is facing."

Attorney Vile complied, but what I heard was much like the teacher from the Charlie Brown comics, "Wonk wonk wonk wonk...".

The entire time she was talking all I could think was, *I can't believe I'm at sentencing being put through trial all over again.*

Then the judge jars me out of my trance by saying, "If you do not admit to being there, I'm going to sentence you to 10 years."

I was hurt and mad at the same time and started to cry.

Then he looks at me and asks, "Would you like me to give you some time to go to the back and think about it?"

Still unable to speak, I nodded my head, "yes."

Attorney Vile and I went to a room in the back of the court. She sat with me about five minutes trying to convince me to admit to what the judge was asking me to do because in her words, "It's in the best interest of your daughter. Think of Morgan. Think of your parents."

She was my attorney, but I really couldn't stand this woman.

Finally, my voice returned, and I said, "No, none of that is true. I wasn't there and saying that I was is not in the best interest of my daughter. Telling the truth is what I want my daughter and my parents to know, not a lie."

She got pissed and walked out.

Next thing I know, in walks a DEA agent trying to beat me down with threats to break me. I told him the same thing I told Attorney Vile, "No, that's not true, and I'm not admitting to it."

Following her lead, he got pissed, and he walked out.

Next, my father walks in and I immediately burst into tears. My father looked at me and in an extremely calm but stern voice he says, "Jessica you must admit to what they are telling you to, or that judge is going to sentence you to ten years."

"But Dad," I cried, "it's a lie."

"I know," Dad said sadly, "but they have the upper hand right now."

I cried harder. I was pissed and hurt at the same time. I took a deep breath and relented, "Ok."

My father left the room and Attorney Vile came in smiling like the snake she was and escorted me back in front of the judge. On the way back to the courtroom we passed the holding area where Michael was.

He called my name and said, "Tell the people what they want to hear. I will be ok."

I cried all the way back to the podium.

Again, the judge said, "You were there the day of the "Jean" transaction?"

I hesitated and then nodded my head, "Yes."

"I need to hear you say yes."

"Yes," I complied.

Countdown To Prison

THE DISREGARD for me and my life was absolutely unnecessary.

"Ms. Roberts," the Judge began, (They didn't recognize my marriage to Michael and insisted on referring to me as Jessica Roberts.) "you must pay for the part you played in this crime." He went into some legal jargon and then continued. "I sentence you to 27 months in Federal prison. You've been through enough already so today I'm going to cut you a break. I'm going to release you on your own recognizance (meaning no bail money is paid to the court, and no bond is posted, the suspect is merely released after promising to appear for upcoming proceedings).

He told me I would be free for 30 days and within that 30-day period, I would receive a letter in the mail instructing me of the date and what prison facility I needed to turn myself into to begin my prison sentence.

Then to add insult to injury, he said, "I don't know what kind of demonic hold Michael has on you and his mother. I can't make you divorce him, but I can separate you two. During your 30-day release, you are not to have any contact with Michael, no visits, no phone calls or letters, and if you violate my order your 30 days will be cut short." Then he said, "Maybe that good name you built for yourself will work in your favor after you serve your prison sentence."

Attorney Vile then decides to speak up on my behalf, "Your Honor, I have here 17 letters written by her co-workers on her behalf. Ms. Roberts is also three weeks away from graduation with her BS degree, and she had an interview lined up for a high salaried job." My jaw just dropped, and I thought to myself, *you should have said all of that during my trial, so the jury could hear*!

I couldn't stand this bitch.

Lastly, Attorney Vile says, "Ms. Roberts would like to do her prison time in a facility in Florida because her mom resides there and will be the caretaker of her daughter when she goes away."

Court was dismissed, and I left the courthouse with my parents.

I passed Kristen's parents as I was leaving, and they stopped me and said, "You keep praying."

I smiled, thanked them and told them I would.

I was the only one out of the five of us sentenced that day who got to go home. The others were taken back to jail to wait to be transported to the prison where they would serve their sentence.

Michael was sentenced to fifteen years, Kristen and Michael's friend both were given ten years, and Michael's mom was sentenced to seven.

I left the courthouse with my parents, and we immediately went to my Aunt Vera's because that's where my Morgan was. I hugged and kissed my Scooterpeas for what seemed like an eternity. She and I were stuck to one another like glue the rest of the day.

News spread quickly that I was out.

The family began stopping by my Aunt's to see me and friends were calling to check on me, but I really wasn't in the mood for answering questions or trying to explain what happened. I was still trying to wrap my mind around it; this was the biggest pill I've ever had to try to swallow in my life, so I was trying not to choke on it so-to-speak.

I really wished that someone would pinch me and wake me from this nightmare.

Nightfall finally arrived, and I made it through my first day of freedom. I slept with Morgan snuggled close to me all night.

The next day I drove to Atlanta to pick up the personal things I'd left in my office. I'd contacted my ex-supervisor to let him know I was coming, and he asked if I wanted him to bring my things out to me because he knew I would be uncomfortable facing my co-workers and all the questions they would have. The three-hour drive to Atlanta gave me some much-needed alone time to think, reflect and accept some things.

I finally arrived at my ex-place of employment and phoned my supervisor to let him know that I'd arrived. He took no time to bring my things out. We chatted briefly, but he didn't ask too many questions because he knew the situation was a sensitive topic. He wished me the best and told me that he would hire me back in a heartbeat once I got this situation behind me. I thanked him and headed back to South Georgia.

During the entire drive back, I was not able to control my thoughts concerning the things that were happening in my life. I decided the best thing for me to do was let things be what they were and focus on controlling my responses and reactions to them.

Two and a half hours later, I arrived back at my Aunt Vera's in South Georgia safe and sound. My mother informed me that she, Morgan and I would be catching the Greyhound to Florida the next day. My father would be leaving tomorrow as well returning to his home in North Carolina.

I spent the rest of my day praying, relaxing and enjoying quality time with my Morgan. Nightfall came, and before bed, I returned a few phone calls from relatives and friends to let them know I was ok. Of course, they wanted details, but I simply replied, "I'm fine, and I do have to serve prison time in 30 days, but if God got me through jail, I know He will do the same when I go to prison."

Each person I made this statement to always replied, "So you're ok? Wow, I thought you would be all broken up about this."

To which I replied, "I have my moments, but overall I'm fine."

The next day we prepare to ride the Greyhound. Greyhound wasn't my preferred way to travel but being that I had nothing but time on my hand, I welcomed it, and the fact that I would be traveling with my two favorite girls (mom and my Morgan) made me happy. It took 14 hours to go from Georgia to Florida via Greyhound, but we finally arrived safely.

The countdown to prison was finally starting to sink in. My prayer to God was to help me remain strong and for God to be with me if I had to go to prison. My entire Florida pre-prison time was dedicated to quality time with my family and lots of isolation time for me to think and pray.

I reflected on the conversation I had with my mom the night before.

"I don't want you coming or bringing Morgan to see me while I'm gone," I said through tears.

"Why not baby?" My mother was crying just as hard as I was.

"It will only be torture for me," I tried to explain. "And I don't want Morgan having any memories of visiting either one of her parents in prison. Promise me Mommie."

"I promise baby, but that's a long time to be without the ones you love."

"We can write and do phone calls," I reasoned. "Besides, you are all in my heart, so I'll never truly be without you."

I knew that my mom would come and bring Morgan as often as I wanted her to, but my mindset was that visits were temporary, and my release would be permanent. Therefore, I could wait.

Although, I was praying and trying to accept my fate, I was hoping that the letter informing me of what prison to turn myself in to would never come or come stating the court has reversed their decision, and I no longer had to serve prison time.

Two weeks into my 30-days of freedom, I received the letter in the mail. I was instructed to report 3 ½ hours away to the Federal Prison Camp in Ocala, Florida, February 28, 2008, by noon. I immediately informed my mom, and although she knew this day was coming, she was shaken and disappointed at the same time. I tried comforting her by telling her I would be fine, "God's got me," I said.

My strength seemed to give her a sense of peace.

I accepted the fact that I had to go through this incarceration and that was no way around it. The next two weeks seemed to fly by and on February 28, 2008, my oldest sister Caroline and her husband, agreed to drive me to the Prison Camp.

I hugged my mom goodbye, and then I hugged and kissed my Morgan which gave me a flashback to the day all of this mess started. I thought about the day the Feds showed up to arrest us, and the female officer pulled Morgan out of my arms. This time it felt like Morgan knew I would be gone much longer. She was crying hysterically. I handed my daughter to my mother as I held back tears. I could hear Morgan crying and screaming all the way outside as I walked to the car.

I was quiet the entire ride to the prison. There were no thoughts running through my mind, just a heavy, hurt heart and a deep out-of-space gaze.

A Foreign Land

WE PULLED UP to the prison, and I took a deep breath, said my goodbyes and walked up to the prison in-take door where I was met by a male jailer who asked for my name and escorted me inside. As we walked in, he asked, "What is a woman like you doing here?"

I didn't respond so he continued, "You wouldn't talk huh?"

Once inside he handed me off to a female jailer who took me inside a room to undress, squat, cough and redress into temporary prison attire until later when I would go to the laundry where I'd pick-up my permanent army-fatigue green prison uniform, boots, etc.

There was a female inmate working in the intake area. She offered me words of encouragement as the jailer told me where I would be housed. The jailer paged for a *big sister* to come and escort me to the unit in which I would be housed.

A *big sister* is a veteran inmate who shows new inmates around the compound and gives them the rundown about where different things are located (i.e., the chow hall, medical, church, recreation, etc.).

Right away I noticed the stark differences between the county jail and federal prison.

At the county jail, I'd felt like a caged animal because of the cell bars and being 'locked in' at night. This is common in jail when it's bed time. County Jail was gated with that 'electric barbed wire' fencing.

In the county, there had been six cells with two people in each cell. The cells were furnished with a cinder block bunk bed with a plastic preschool mat as the mattress, a toilet, and a shower. The cell I was in had a small window.

We were not allowed to go outside, but instead, we went to what was called 'recreation' which was just an empty room where you could walk, exercise, or play games.

We were allowed to attend church (a room with chairs and an outside minister to conduct the services).

I was in the county jail for three months and 21 days before I was back in court for sentencing.

Jail wasn't scary to me.

It was like I was in a foreign land because this was my first time. All the ladies around me had been here several times, so I couldn't relate to them, and they couldn't understand me.

There were arguments and fights, but nothing violent where weapons were used.

The food was extremely nasty, but from time to time there were a couple of meals that were edible. I purchased items from the canteen store, which was mostly junk (chips, cookies, honey buns, etc.) and that's how I survived. I ate really bad in jail because there weren't many options.

The whole time I was in the county jail, I only had one roommate who as I said earlier, ended up being on my case with me.

Federal Prison Camp was entirely different from the county jail atmosphere.

There were no cells, and the Camp wasn't gated. There were these big rocks in strategic places around the camp lawn that we (inmates) were prohibited from passing. Ironically, there was more freedom at the Prison Camp.

There was a salon (I got my hair permed, colored, and cut just like I did when I was free.) Payment for this was secured by purchasing the stylist the items she requested from the canteen store.

The canteen store had many more items to purchase than jail. There were shoes, jewelry, food and a variety of other things. Even the food was better than the food at the county jail.

Of course, there were more inmates here, but we got to go outside as we pleased until curfew.

I had three different roommates throughout my entire prison stay. The rooms were cubicle styled and had bunk beds with real mattresses. There were two people assigned to each room.

Each housing unit had three TV rooms and four desktop computers (for emailing but couldn't include pictures). There was volleyball, a track for running or walking and a recreation room where you could watch movies. We were allowed to take classes too. There was even a prison choir!

Yes, there were always arguments and fights, but nothing like you see portrayed on TV. The guards weren't having that.

Some of the talented ladies in prison even hosted birthday celebrations with elaborately themed décor!

Prison wasn't scary for me either. I just didn't want to be there. But I made the best of it by working and being positive and productive with my time.

The first day was hard for me. Words can't express how hard it was being away from my daughter and my family. I didn't want them to see me in prison. In my opinion, it would make doing my time harder. It would cause me to be impatient about being released which would have made me depressed and miserable.

Although I missed everyone dearly, I felt that lots of visits would have only been torture for me.

I received lots of letters and books instead.

Cassidy and I wrote each other often. She kept me informed on what was going on. She listened to me when I was weak and complained, and instead of participating in the pity party, she encouraged me and made me laugh. She let me know that it was ok to feel sad, but that I couldn't remain that way. I had to stay focused for my daughter as well as for myself.

So, I used the computer and kept in touch with my family. I made that be more than enough.

The first day of my prison stay was spent with my *big sister* until it was time to return to my housing unit for the night.

As I lay there that first night, my thoughts were of Morgan. I missed her terribly. I missed cooking for her and bathing her and tucking her in at night before bed.

This place was not my final destination. I was only a visitor, and if I stayed positive and focused, I'd get to go home in no time.

I wanted to remain a foreigner here. I refused to allow myself to become accustomed to this life.

The Grace Of God

THE NEXT DAY CAME, and I realized I had made it through better than I expected.

My *big sister* stopped by the cube (where I slept) to show me where the laundry was so I could pick up my permanent uniform, boots, jacket, etc. On our way out the door, we were approached by the jailer in charge of the unit where I was housed, and he informed us that there was a floor buffering job available and asked if we knew anyone interested. My *big sister* looked at me and asked if I interested because she said, "Unless you have a documented medical condition, you have to have a job."

"I'm interested," I replied. "But I've never buffed a floor before."

"That's fine," she said. "I'll teach you."

And just like that on the second day of my incarceration, I had a job that I didn't have to look for; it found me.

My *big sister* and I made our way to the laundry where I picked up my items. It was time for her to go to work so now it was time for me to get familiar with my surroundings without a tour guide.

I decided to check my account to see if my mom had put money in it. And she had so I decided to go shopping at the commissary store. While waiting on my commissary order to be filled, I met an older lady who told me she had been at the prison for fifteen months and was going home in two weeks.

"Congratulations," I said genuinely happy for her. "How did you do it?"

"By the grace of God," she said simply.

I thought to myself, *27 months is so far away but if that older lady can do it and remain sane, I can too.*

The next morning, I learned how to buff the waxed concrete floors in my housing unit. After about thirty minutes I was left on my own to buff the entire housing unit. It took me a little over two hours to buff the entire unit. Once I was done the jailer in charge of the housing unit complemented me on the great job I'd done.

As weeks went by, I became more familiar with the classes and activities the Prison camp had to offer. I decided to get involved in a few activities to keep busy to help the time pass. *The busier I am,* I thought, *the quicker the time will pass.*

I enrolled in a couple of courses, attended church, watched movies in the recreation center, walked the track daily and watched spiritual sermons in the chapel movie room.

After 30 days in prison, I realized I'd survived. I missed my Morgan like crazy, but I had survived.

The inmate worker who worked in receiving whom I met during my in-take approached me and told me she was being released in a week and asked if I would be interested in being her replacement in receiving. I didn't hesitate to tell her I was interested.

I immediately informed the jailer over the housing unit of my new job. He understood and didn't give me any grief.

And the next day, I started my new gig.

I was now the orderly in the receiving and departure area responsible for delivering in-house mail to the other prison facilities (there were four male prisons located in the same area as the camp) via golf cart or a government vehicle if it rained.

As word spread that I had gotten this job, there were a few people upset because they thought the job should have been given to someone with more seniority.

I didn't let the grumbling distract me. I knew this job was a blessing and I loved it because it made my days go fast. It was a split shift job. I would go in the mornings and do my orderly duties which took an hour to an hour and a half. Then I would go do whatever I wanted and after lunch, return to work to do the mail delivery which took a couple of hours.

My mindset coming into to prison was to do my time quietly, so no one would know who I was; where I was from, etc., etc. but this job made me known all over the compound. So much for being incognito.

Six months into my prison stint, and it had been uneventful for me up until the day my roommate's girlfriend decides to come to our cube and start an argument with her.

"I don't want to hear all that noise," I said calmly. "Yall need to take that outside."

Of course, the girlfriend mumbled something as she walked away.

"What did you say?" I asked.

She kept on walking. They argued frequently, and generally, I kept out of it since it was none of my business, until they decided to bring the drama to our cube.

The next week they got into a huge physical fight, and they both got shipped to different prison facilities. Other than that small incident, I was doing my time well and without incident.

Shortly after that, I received word that Michael's mom passed away in prison from a bad fall that she never recovered from. She had been sickly prior to going to prison. This was a shock and a hard pill to swallow. This news was by far, the worst news I received my entire time being incarcerated.

Ten months into my sentence, my counselor informed me that my three months halfway house time would now be doubled to six months, which meant I would only serve 18 months in prison and the remaining six months of my sentence in a halfway house. (18 months in prison, six months in a halfway house and 3 months in the county equal the 27-month sentence.)

This meant I now had less than a year to finish out my prison time and I was super excited!

My counselor informed me that I needed to provide her with an address where I would go once, I was released from the halfway house. I told her I would have one to her by the end of the week. I phoned a couple of people I knew who would allow me to live with them temporarily.

Initially, each person told me, yes, but when I told them that my probation officer would have to pay them a visit prior to my release to make sure that the residence was safe, drug-free, etc. each person changed their mind and said no they didn't want the authorities invading their privacy. I told each of them that I understood, but I was really crushed on the inside. I mean all the things I'd done to help others and now that I'm in need, I'm turned down by the two people that I thought I could depend on.

I've always helped others out of the goodness of my heart expecting nothing in return, but I was really disappointed and surprised when my list of *go-to* people wasn't a list at all. I had no choice but to use Michael's brother's address. He didn't hesitate when I called him and asked. I thanked him and told him I would keep him posted of my official release date.

Michael's brother lived in South Georgia, and I did not want to live in South Georgia, I wanted to return to Atlanta, but I had no choice at this time. The end of the week arrived, and I gave my Counselor my release address, which was Michael's brother Ben's address).

Fourteen months into my prison sentence, I get my first visit from my mom, Morgan, my younger sister, and her daughter. I was so excited because it was a contact visit. I would get to hold, hug and kiss on my Morgan. My Morgan had grown so much. She was just as excited to see me as I was to see her. It was a great visit.

Mom and my sister couldn't believe the variety of women in prison. They were all different ages, races and in for all different types of things. Mom and my sister also couldn't believe how nice the women looked.

"We have a salon in here," I said and laughed. "Some of the women in here used to be stylists before being sent to prison."

We laughed, talked and ate vending machine food until the visit was over. I was happy to see them come but sad to see them go.

The next month I received a visit from Joy, a long-time high school friend of mine who currently resided in another state but was coming to Florida to visit her parents. I was excited to see her and overjoyed that she went out of her way to visit me. We had a great visit.

What was significant about her visit, and something I will never forget is how she thought enough of me to ask if she could visit. Only my family knew of my preference for limited visits. There were people that I knew who lived in the area or close to the area who never even asked to visit me.

The final month of my incarceration arrived, and it was time to prepare for my release to the halfway house.

My counselor informed me of my release date and told me that I would be doing my halfway house time at the Federal Halfway House in Savannah, Georgia. I phoned my mom and told her of the good news and asked if she would send me some release clothes. Mom was excited. She agreed and said, "Jessica baby, it's almost over."

I told my jailer supervisor, and to my surprise, she wasn't happy that I was leaving.

"I think you should do your halfway house time here," she said.

"No," I said frowning. "I'm ready to go home."

"You will regret going to the halfway house," she warned. "I've never heard anything good about those facilities."

"If I can make it through prison," I said confidently. "I can most definitely survive a halfway house."

Listening To The Spirit

ON THE DAY of my release, Michael's brother Ben and his wife drove down from South Georgia to pick me up and take me to Savannah Georgia where the halfway house was. I was excited and nervous. The drive took about five hours, but we finally arrived safely.

I checked in, and Ben and his wife left.

I was really shocked to see both men and women in the Halfway house; it was a co-ed facility. The next day I met with my counselor, and she informed me of the rules and regulations. They didn't make things easy.

I had to take the city bus to look for a job Monday through Friday. I've never had to use public transportation before because I've always had a car. When out looking jobs, the protocol was to have an employee of the company initial a form confirming you completed an application for employment. I also had to ask if I could use the phone to let the halfway house know where I was and when I was leaving to go to the next business to look for work.

This was a very humiliating experience. Most of the businesses denied use of their phone and refused to sign the form. Eventually after several complaints from businesses and halfway residents the phone call requirement and form signing was done away with. The new requirement was to list the business you visited each day and the time in and out.

Not only was looking for jobs hard, dealing with the female halfway house staff was difficult as well. For instance, I was told when I attended church on Sunday's via a church pass; I was required to have the Pastor or his wife sign a form confirming my attendance. My church pass was only 2 hours and most of the time church was still going on when it was time for me to leave.

The male halfway house staff never required this humiliating task.

When I was told this by female staff, I said to myself *I'll just have the friend I attend church with to sign because they won't know the difference anyway.*

After about 2 weeks of looking for a job, I gained employment at a well-known Hotel as a housekeeper which was a first for me, but as I've always done with any job I've had, I applied my impeccable work ethic.

I was excited to be working. Fifty dollars was deducted out of my pay every week to cover my stay in the Halfway house. I used the rest of my money to buy hygiene products, food (I refused to eat the food that was catered/donated because I saw a huge cockroach crawl from one of the delivery containers one day) and get my hair done which I considered a necessity.

I got my hair styled by the best hair stylist in Savannah, Peggy. Peggy was shapely, extremely talented at what she did, but what drew me to her the most was her kind heart and her strong will and determination. She too was an overcomer.

About a month into being employed at the Hotel, myself and Alice, another resident of the Halfway house, got into an argument on the job. I let Alice use my room access card to unlock one of the rooms she was responsible for cleaning with the understanding that she would return it as soon as she unlocked the room door. I finished cleaning the room that I was working on and 15 minutes passed before I decided to go and look for Alice.

I became upset because I couldn't clean my next room because Alice had my key. When I finally found her, I let her know how I didn't appreciate her not returning my key, and one word leads to another, and before I knew it, I was in a full-fledged argument while customers watched. The customers reported Alice and me to management, and we both were suspended for three days. Tonya, our manager, told us she would not report our suspension to the Halfway house, so we could just tell them we had the next three days off from work because they were cutting back on hours.

The next day I decided to get my hair done since I had the next three days off but before I left for the salon something in my spirit told me to tell the Halfway Lead about the argument with Alice and the resulting suspension. I reassured the Lead that the situation was over, and she didn't have to worry about Alice and me having words again. The lead said she was shocked that Tonya (the hotel manager) told us not to report the incident.

I arrived at the salon and noticed that Peggy's Shampoo Tech wasn't there. I inquired with Peggy as to Shampoo Tech's whereabouts, and Peggy informed me that she no longer worked there. I thought to myself, *hmmm I wonder if she would hire me.*

And before the thought disappeared, Peggy asked me where I was working (she knew I was in the Halfway house) and I told her at a Hotel, but I was suspended for three days. Peggy then asked me if I was interested in the shampoo tech position. I immediately replied yes!!!! She and I discussed and worked out the particulars. One of the perks that came with my new job was free hair-dos. I couldn't wait to get back to the Halfway house to get official approval.

I arrived at the Halfway house and immediately told the lead about my job offering at the salon. She congratulated me and gave her approval. I asked did I need to give the hotel notice, but she replied no.

The weekend arrived, and I was going on my first home visit to Michael's brother Ben's house. I was excited to be getting back into the swing of life outside of prison. I spent the entire weekend at Ben's and knew in my heart I did not want to live there once released from the halfway house.

Sunday even came quickly, and I headed back to the halfway house. I would start my new job at the salon on Tuesday and so decided to spend Monday finding a different residence of release from the Halfway house. As I pondered on who to contact, it dawned on me to check with Stacy and Tyrone.

Stacy and Tyrone were a young, loving couple with big hearts. I'd known them for several years. They lived in Atlanta and would probably allow me to live with them temporarily. I phoned them and told them of my release dilemma and made them aware that my probation officer would have to visit their residence if they agreed to me being released to their address. They agreed that I could live with them until I got on my feet, which we all thought would take about a year. I was so excited. I completed a new release form immediately.

Later that evening one of the halfway house residents who worked at the Hotel told me that Tonya (the hotel manager) was pissed that I had quit because I was a good worker and didn't notify her. Tonya also stated since I shitted on her, she was going to shit on me by contacting the Halfway house and telling the Lead about Alice and my argument and that she had suspended the both of us for three days.

I shook my head and smiled because I had already informed the Lead. I thought to myself *I'm glad I listen to my spirit, Jesus saves!*

Tuesday morning came fast, and I was so excited. It was my first day working at the salon. Before I left for the salon, the halfway lead called me into her office and told me that Tonya (Hotel Manager) called her and told her of the argument and suspension. To which the Lead told me she simply replied, "Jessica has already told me everything." The Lead and I laughed.

The next three months in the Halfway house went smoothly. I was enjoying working at the salon. The owner Peggy even gave me a key to the building, and I was approved to work extended hours. I also was approved to have my vehicle which, my nephew delivered to me.

Lastly, I was approved for home confinement with an ankle monitor.

My mother's youngest sister lives in Savannah, and she allowed me to live out my last three months of Halfway house via home confinement with her and her family. My day of release for home confinement arrived, and the Halfway house was out of ankle monitors.

I thought to myself thank God because I really didn't want to have to deal with the stares and questions from people, etc. I was also required to have a separate landline installed at my aunt's home.

My life seemed to be getting some normalcies to it. I must admit as it got closer to my last 30 days, I was getting a bit nervous because I didn't know what to expect once I relocated back to Atlanta.

My final Friday working in the salon and being in the Halfway house/home confinement finally arrived. I was excited to sign my halfway house release papers. Peggy (salon owner) treated me to lunch.

Leaving Peggy was hard. She and I had formed a genuine friendship. I was really going to miss her, our before and after work talks and all the laughs, etc. that we shared.

Saturday morning arrived, and as I traveled back to my favorite place, Atlanta, my thoughts were on how to rebuild my life.

I thought to myself, *how in the world I'm I going to put my life back together; get my daughter back from my mom so that she and I can live a normal life again?*

I finally arrived in Atlanta, and it felt good but different. I felt at home but lost at the same time.

I pulled up to Stacy and Tyrone's home and was in awe of how beautiful it was. I felt very honored that they agreed to let me live with them temporarily. I was as happy to see them as they were me. We sat and chatted for the rest of the evening. They told me that my Probation officer had visited the week before and she was very pleased with their home and with them and felt me residing with them was good and safe.

Monday morning arrived, and it was time to get down to business. Looking for a job was first on my list of priorities. Tyrone referred me to Danny, a friend of his who owned a Temp Employment Agency. I met with Danny and explained my situation, and to my surprise, Danny agreed to help me find employment. I started work at a warehouse the following week, a part-time data entry position making $9.00 per hour. Although, this would be my first time working in a warehouse and the pay was $9.50 less than I was making before incarceration, I was grateful.

This is just temporary, I told myself. *I have to start somewhere.*

My first day on the job went well and to top it off the company was a Christian-based warehouse which I thought was unique because religion of any sort was normally not talked about in your place of employment. I worked side-by-side with a trainer for a few days more and then was released to work alone. I was trained to do data entry, pallet wrapping, sorting, etc. My co-workers could tell I was new to the warehouse world, but after a couple months I was wrapping pallets and handling the pallet jack like a champ.

The data entry part of my job came natural, but once I got the hang of the pallet jack and wrapping pallets, I even impressed myself.

After about three months, I was offered a permanent part-time position with the warehouse which I had to complete an official job application. I was excited about the offer but skeptical about completing the application because I knew I would have to address my criminal background. I told a co-worker of my dilemma, and she suggested that I lie on the application and mark "no" to the criminal background question.

"But if I lie," I reasoned, "and they find out I won't get hired on and they will feel I can't be trusted."

"If I were you," she said simply, "I would lie."

I spent the rest of my evening thinking about how I should handle the situation. Finally, I decided to pray about it and give it to God. The next day I awoke and prepared for my workday, and my spirit spoke to me and led me to have a conversation with my warehouse supervisor before I completed the application.

When I arrived to work, I approached my Supervisor and asked if he had a moment to speak with me privately. I gave my Supervisor the short version of my criminal background, and to my surprise, his response was, "Jessica I'm sorry that happened to you, but I'm not judging you based on your past. You have an impeccable work ethic and are an asset to the company." Next, he says, "I appreciate your honesty and want to hire you regardless of your past." He then explained to me that the Company uses a third party to conduct the TSA background checks and he will contact them to tell them my situation and inform them that he still wants to hire me. Finally, he adds, "Jessica I'm glad you came to talk with me because if you had answered the criminal background question dishonestly, I wouldn't have hired you."

I smiled, thanked him and worked the rest of my day with a clear conscious. My thoughts on my drive home from work were, *although things aren't easy for me right now, I thank God for humbling me and revealing the lessons I need to see and learn along my journey.*

Re-Entry

WORKING AT THE WAREHOUSE was going well, but I began to apply for jobs and positions in my field of interest. I was landing interviews left and right with successful, well-known Corporations, but every time they got to the question on the application about my criminal background, and I answered it honestly and provided an explanation, the interview process seem to get cold, stale and end abruptly with the Interviewer stating, "Our policy prohibits hiring persons with a criminal history."

I was brought to tears in the midst of some of the interviews while trying to provide an explanation of my incarceration. Sometimes there would be one interviewer, and sometimes there would be a panel of interviewers. They would listen to my story very intently, but it never worked in my favor.

Any free time I had, I spent looking for better employment and organizations that helped people in my situation who were formerly incarcerated. I researched (online) and attended countless events, expos, conferences, training, meetings, etc. for ex-felons/ individuals with criminal backgrounds but at the end of each event the only thing I received was a certificate (sometimes) and a list of companies that *supposedly* hired ex-felons (this list seemed to be popular at every event). At the end of each event, I attended I never received any *real* help, just more information that left me on my own doing more research. I even got bonded in hopes that it would increase my chances of gaining better employment.

Michael's brother Ben came into some money and hired an Appeal attorney for us. And the Appeal Attorney assured me that my case would be overturned, and we would be able to sue for the injustice I received. He told me in all his years of practicing law he had never witnessed such an upset/displeasing response from Judges who listened to an appeal argument as he did with mine. He also mentions that one of the Judges made a statement as to how was Jessica convicted and sent to prison with no evidence. It took a couple of weeks to hear back from our Appeal attorney that we (Michael, his mom and I) lost the Appeal. I was disappointed but not surprised because of what I'd personally witness from the so-called Justice system, and at this point, I was well on my way to rebuilding my life.

One of the training sessions I attended for felons I was afforded the opportunity to have a one-on-one with the guy in charge, Mr. Jeffers. I gave him the short version of what happened to me. He listened to me very intently, but once I was done talking, he spoke. He said, "Jessica I'm going to speak to you off the record right now."

"Ok," I replied.

He stood up and closed his office door and said to me in a very serious, stern voice, "I want you to stop making damn excuses for him right now. I listened to everything you said, and all you did was make excuses for your daughter's father. He's a coward; a real man would never allow his woman or his mother to go to prison."

As he continued to speak the truth, I could do nothing but listen and cry because everything he was saying to me I needed to hear. And I needed to hear it just like he gave it to me, raw and uncut.

I didn't leave this training with a job. I left with something more which was a reality check. I thought to myself, *why hadn't anyone close to me ever spoke to me as Mr. Jeffers did.*

I really needed that, not the sympathy that everyone seems to give me.

From that day forward thoughts of my future included Morgan and me, not Michael.

After being in Atlanta for seven months, Tyrone and Stacy told me that they would be getting married. I was super excited for them because they'd been together for some time now, so marriage for them was a good thing.

The initial plan was for me to reside with Tyrone and Stacy for a year, but I had no idea I would have such a hard time finding a job. I never thought in a million years I would still be working at the warehouse. I reassured Stacy and Tyrone that I would be moved out by the time they got married which was three months away.

I contacted my mother and told her about my dilemma. She told me that she would be willing to move to Atlanta to help me out until I got a better job. This was music to my ears. I would have Morgan back with me sooner than I thought. Mom told me to look for a nice, comfortable place for her, I and Morgan to live. She also told me to contact my father and ask if he would help us financially with moving expenses.

My father agreed to help us.

I continued working at the warehouse, searching for better employment, looking for a place for mom, Morgan & I to live and attending any event that claims to offer help to ex-felons.

Three months later, I found a nice townhome for mom, Morgan and myself. I moved out of Stacy, and Tyrone's home the Friday before their wedding. I had a few friends help me move my furniture from storage into my new place. My goal was to have our new place all set up, and all would be left for me to do was fly to Florida to get mom and Morgan. I attended Stacy and Tyrone's wedding that Saturday which was a beautiful ceremony.

The next day I traveled to Florida via plane to get mom and Morgan. This would be my first-time seeing Morgan and mom since being out of prison. I arrived in Florida safely and couldn't wait to hold my precious Morgan. Morgan and mom were at my oldest sister's home. Mom met me at the door giving me a huge hug.

I step inside the door, and everyone was laughing. They said Morgan had run to hide. A few minutes later Morgan comes running from the back. I reached down to hug her and pick her up with tears of joy streaming down my face. I couldn't believe how much she had grown. Words can't explain how good it felt holding my Morgan.

I drove myself, mom and Morgan, back to Atlanta in mom's car the next day. Morgan and mom loved our new place. It didn't take long for them to get settled in.

Three months after moving into our new place, I finally get a breakthrough. I get a better job in my field with better pay. I passed the background check for this job thank God. I was super excited. I'd worked at the warehouse for a year prior to starting my new job. Things were slowly, but surely getting back to normal.

Michael had started writing me letters to which I never wrote back. My attitude was I'm trying to make a living to provide for Morgan and I. I've done my time in prison, and I refuse to do his via the commands, demands, etc. he was requesting through his letters. Me not writing him back didn't stop him from writing, and his letters got more hateful and full of nothing but anger, threats, and negativity as time went on.

I eventually stop opening the letters and just stacked them in a shoe box. I had to remain positive and focused, so I didn't have time to entertain Michael's foolishness. I became stronger mentally and spiritually as time passed.

One day I received a call from the CEO of a Re-Entry Organization for female ex-offenders inviting me to attend a meeting. Truth be told I'd been receiving email invites from this Organization for a year, but I always ignored the invite. I gave the CEO my word that I would attend the meeting. I figured what the heck, I'd attending tons of meetings, etc. for Re-Entry without being personally invited, this could be the one I've been looking for.

Saturday came, and I attended the Re-Entry meeting and learned the organization mentored formally incarcerated and incarcerated and provided resource referrals for jobs, housing, etc. The meeting consisted of a group of women sharing their stories and providing tools and discussion topics to help with the healing process. The organization also did street outreach, advocating on behalf of incarceration and the injustice in the Justice system, etc.

After a few weeks of attendance, I became an official member.

Epilogue

TWO YEARS AFTER my release from prison, I decided to go back to school and complete my B.S. degree which I did in less than a year. And immediately afterward, I enrolled in school to obtain my MBA degree which took me a little over a year and a half to complete because I enrolled in an accelerated degree program.

Education afforded me with a new and better job with the same company I worked for prior to the incarceration but in a different department. After being in that department for only three months, I was promoted to a different position in the same department. I worked this position for about six months before being promoted again; this time to a higher salaried position in a different department.

Things were looking up for me.

My daughter was thriving and hadn't experienced any negative fallout from my incarceration. As a matter of fact, she doesn't recall much of it. She was 4 ½ when I was released. She doesn't remember the daily phone calls (sometimes multiple times a day), but I do. I first heard her tell me she loved me over the phone, while I was in county jail. She was just learning to talk. She would always laugh when I called her all the pet names I had for her, so I know she knew it was her mom.

Morgan had been told that I had gone to jail for a speeding ticket. I let her believe that until she was nine and that's when I told her the real story. It was only by God's grace and mercy that our bond wasn't affected and that she didn't suffer any mental damage from the experience. If you saw her today, you would never know her parents were ever away from her.

When my Mom saw that things were getting better for me career wise, she decided it was time for her to move back to Florida. Although I hated to see her go, I knew that she preferred living in Florida and only moved to Atlanta to help me until I got on my feet.

I continued to participate heavily in Re-Entry events, activities, etc. via the Re-Entry Organization. I was even asked to be a board member and eventually was named the CFO (Chief Financial Officer) of the organization. I began to make a name for myself because of my active re-entry participation, which include the following:

- I was afforded the opportunity to be a guest on a podcast radio show.
- I was invited to share my story during a listening session of attorneys and advocates which was videoed.
- I hosted an internet radio show for a short period of time.

- I created *Speak On It* which is a Facebook blog that partners with a radio show out of Florida.
- I mentor females at the Federal Halfway house.
- I mentor females at one of the local jails in Atlanta.

In 2016, I decided that it was time for me to separate myself from Michael legally. I filed for divorce.

Of course, he was upset with my decision and did things to try to stop it; that hurt me. He wrote letters assassinating my character and calling me an unfit mother to my divorce attorney and the Judge assigned to our divorce case. I equipped myself with all the threating, negative letters he had written me and together with the letters he wrote my attorney and the judge, it became clear who was the real unfit parent (him).

Michael had been in prison for almost ten years by then and still it seemed he had not humbled himself or changed for the better. I had to protect myself and Morgan from his toxicity. I never breathe a bad or negative word to Morgan about her father even though he tried his best to hurt me from behind prison walls.

When Morgan asked questions about her father, I answered them. My mindset was I would take the blows from Michael and not allow them to affect my child. Over time, I'd become spiritually and emotionally sound, so much so, that the things that Michael said or did not pierce my spirit.

When our court date finally came, I was strong and prepared.

Michael requested to be transported from prison via the local Sheriff, so he could attend our divorce hearing in person, but the Judge denied his request. It took the judge seven minutes to grant the divorce, full custody of Morgan to me and restore me to my maiden name. I left the courtroom thinking; *it pays to be humble and allow God to fight your battles.*

I wasn't angry with Michael; I just didn't want anything to do with him other than for him to be a father to our Morgan and for us to be cordial to one another so that we could have a functional co-parenting relationship.

A year after the divorce, I found out through the grapevine that Michael had been released from prison. I was shocked and immediately made an appointment with the child support office. I figured allowing the court to handle our situation was best because of how Michael conducted himself during our divorce proceedings.

I arrived at the Child Support office to begin the process and was told that I couldn't proceed until Michael was released from the halfway house. I was disappointed at this news but set a reminder via my cell phone calendar to remind me when it was time to try again.

A few weeks later I was at home looking in the mirror putting the finishing touches to my makeup when my Spirit spoke to me and said, "Call him, don't put the court in it."

I tried ignoring it, but then I heard, "Obedience is better than sacrifice." I stopped what I was doing and just stood there for a few minutes thinking to myself, *but my plan is to deal with him as less as possible.*

Obedience won. I gathered myself and phoned Michael.

He answered, and I said, "I didn't call to argue." I told him what had just been placed in my spirit to do, and that I had to be obedient. "As long as we can be cordial with one another and do what's in the best interest of Morgan," I continued. "I will not put child support or the court in our situation. I've had enough of court and the legal system."

Michael agreed, and we've been co-parenting and being friends ever since.

Unbeknownst to me Michael received counseling soon after our divorce, prior to his release from prison and was now a changed man working on bettering himself.

Once again, I'm glad I listened to my spirit.

Michael and I discussed how best to move forward and decided that it would be a good idea for

Morgan to spend Thanksgiving with him. My intention was never to keep Morgan away from Michael. I was eager for him to visit with her over the Thanksgiving holiday. I wanted him to see first-hand that I had not poisoned Morgan against him.

"So how do you feel about seeing your dad," I ask cautiously. Thanksgiving was only a few weeks away and I wanted to be sure my daughter was prepared.

"I'm excited," she says. "I forgive him for the bad choices he made. I'm ready to start spending time with him," she continued.

In that moment, I was so proud of my one and only, beautiful, smart daughter. Although she was only eleven at the time, she somehow had managed the art of forgiveness. That's something not too many people can accomplish after a lifetime of living.

Morgan truly is amazing. She is the love of my life.

As we embrace, I notice that not only has she gotten taller and wiser, but now I could see both Michael and me in her. She is the best of us all wrapped up in one person.

"Come here Scooterpeas and give your mom a hug," I say trying to hold back tears. "I'm going to miss you while you're gone."

The day soon came for Morgan to go with her father. When Michael arrived to pick her up, they hugged one another as if he had never been away; it was genuinely happy and welcoming. Me seeing that Morgan was not afraid, gave me comfort and peace of mind. I kissed Morgan and told them to have fun.

By 2018, my career was flourishing, I've forgiven Michael and we are co-parents as well as friends. I'm a mentor, *Speak On It* is now two years old and expanding with the radio station, and now I'm an Author!

The road to piecing my life back together hasn't been easy because the higher GOD elevates me, the more some try to sabotage, distract, character assassinate, dim my light, and envy my strength. But I survived and didn't give up. The fire inside of me burns brighter than the fires around me.

I used the bricks that were thrown at me along my journey as stepping stones to stand on, to aide me in solidifying my foundation as I pursued greatness. I refused to let those people take away or destroy what God implanted in me. I discovered my God-given purpose by allowing my *Tragedy* to mature into *Triumph*.

I'm well on my way to achieving my ultimate goal, CEO of a company that assists women/females with troubled pasts.

I am triumphant!

Triumphant!

Discussion Questions

Does doing right and being good guarantee that you won't have trouble in your life?

Do you see a pattern in Jessica's life? If so, what is it?

Why do you think Jessica was attracting the same types of men in her life?

Why do you think Jessica chose not to save herself when her attorney kept trying to get her to talk to the DEA Agents?

Do you feel Jessica's attitude and demeanor toward her attorney (Vile) was right?

Do you think Jessica's loving, sound family upbringing influenced her life positively or negatively?

Do you think Jessica married Michael because she loved him or because of the situation?

Do you feel that Jessica should have stood her ground and not allowed Michael's father to live with them after his release from prison?

If you were in Jessica's shoes would you have made the same choice(s)? Why or why not?

Triumphant!

"Why do we hold onto negativity?
For some reason,
we believe that others are affected
by our experience of remaining upset, hurt or
angry. Holding on to pain, anger, guilt or shame
is the glue that binds us to the situation
we want to escape."

~ *Iyanla Vanzant*

"What tried to demolish me,
I allowed to polish me."

-India Arie

PHOTO GALLERY

Photo 1: Bachelor of Science Degree -
Technical Management, "Human
Resources"

Photo 2: MBA Degree - Human Resource Management

*Photo 3: MBA Degree - Human Resource
Management*

Photo 4: Shyla as a baby

Photo 5: Author Jessica Roberts and daughter Shyla

Photo 6: Shyla

Photo 7: Author Jessica Roberts at work

Photo 8: Barbara Arnwine: Igniting the Change podcast radio show

Link to the podcast show:

http://barbaraarnwine.com/todays-show/jessica-alvin/

Photo 9a (Speak on It Facebook blog/partnered with FL radio host Jumpin Joe

Photo 9b: WEBS Radio Show

Photo 10 Dismas Halfway House Certificate:
Volunteer mentor to female residents

Triumphant!

About the Author

Jessica Roberts was raised in a two-parent home. She is the middle child of three (two sisters) and grew up in a middle-class household. Her mother and father both worked outside of the home, which afforded the family a comfortable lifestyle.

Her parents were committed to their children and instilled in them the concepts of high morals, values, independence, responsibility and a strong/firm work ethic.

Prior to October 2007 (the whole drug conspiracy ordeal), the author's life was happy. She was a proud and responsible first-time mom to her beautiful little girl. She was also gainfully employed at a well-known Company.

With only three weeks away from graduating with a Bachelor of Science in Human Resource Management (she was unable to complete due to being arrested and sentenced to prison), Jessica was on the fast track to success having landed an interview for a higher salaried government contract position due to take place once she returned from court (again, this didn't happen because of being sentenced to jail and prison).

The author cites her role in the drug conspiracy case and subsequent indictment was due to her relationship with her daughter's father and the people with whom he associated.

The criminal case that Jessica was part of consisted of a 38-person indictment with her being number 38. According to her hired attorney, she wasn't granted an evidentiary hearing because there was no evidence against her. Her entire involvement in the case hinged on the DEA *thinking* she knew something but wasn't telling it.

Having had no prior criminal record, the entire ordeal was emotionally and physically traumatic. Jessica's life took a complete turn away from the direction in which she was headed.

In short, a once promising life was now reduced to a ten-year federal prison sentence. Thankfully, after unimaginable judicial system torture and lies, she was actually sentenced to 27 months in a Federal Prison Camp, 5 years of probation and a $5,000 fine.

By God's grace and her morally sound upbringing, the experience made her better not bitter.

The road to piecing her life back together hasn't been easy but she continues to accomplish her goals.

A few of her accomplishments include:

- MBA in Human Resource Management
- BS in Technical Management with an emphasis in Human Resources
- Employment with a successful Corporation

- Small Business Development Training Certificate of Completion (Univ of Georgia)
- A plethora of on-the-job-training in various software / systems
- Chief Financial Officer and a board member of *The Re-Entry Connection* (a non-profit organization that mentors ex-female offenders)
- Guest on the *Igniting for Change* Podcast with Barbara Arwine
- Creator of *Speak On It with Jessica Nicole* (A Facebook blog page that has an on-air segment with Jumping Joe Jenkins: WJFP radio-FL)
- Volunteer/mentor to female resident at Federal Halfway house in Atlanta, GA
- Volunteer/mentor to female resident at local jails in Atlanta, GA

The author's ultimate goal is to be CEO/Owner/Operator of a company that assist women/ females with troubled pasts.

Black Gold

When you are gifted Jessica, you attract all kinds. That's why you *gotta* protect yourself and Shyla.

When a flower blooms and releases its fragrance, she is not alone because her fragrance is exuding energy and as a result, the bees are coming to withdraw from her nectar.

This metaphor I'm using is to show you a parallel of how your gifts and talents, strength and beauty are attracting bees, but never forget those bees have fighting mechanisms to defend themselves when they feel they are in danger. Any subtle movement generates a defensive reaction. Without them discerning a real threat, they just get defensive.

As a result, the flower has to rely on the Creator and other creation for her existence.

But each time you are crushed hopefully your wisdom, knowledge, and understanding is increasing to greater degrees.

I'm sure just as well as myself, there's a book in you that could save someone's life in crisis.

Your words are strong, thought-provoking, and engaging. Don't ever sleep in your worth.

You are the mother of civilization, the caregiver of all mankind. You are indicative of the beauty of all that is bright in the day and the calm repose of the darkness, stars, and moon at night.

You are a breath of fresh air upon the faces of all those awaiting.

YOU ARE BLACK GOLD; YOU ARE QUEEN!!!

-Kingzown

(printed by permission)

BLACK BUTTERFLY BOOKS

is an imprint of

The Butterfly Typeface Publishing.

Contact us for all your

publishing & writing needs!

Iris M Williams

PO Box 56193

Little Rock AR 72215

www.butterflytypeface.com

Made in the USA
Columbia, SC
09 March 2019